60 Year Journey with Lambretta

Dick Sedgley

60 Year Journey with Lambretta

Olympia Publishers
London

www.olympiapublishers.com

OLYMPIA PAPERBACK EDITION

A CIP catalogue record for this title is
available from the British Library.

ISBN: 978-1-78830-668-3

First Published in 2021

Olympia Publishers
Tallis House
2 Tallis Street
London
EC4Y 0AB
Printed in Great Britain

INTRODUCTION

This book is about my life with Lambretta Scooters, and working as a mechanic in the Service Department at Lambretta Concessionaires Limited, Croydon, Surrey, becoming friends and working with the late Mike Karslake — from time to time — and restoring my scooters until the present day.

My scooter interest probably started back in my school days. I would cycle for miles at weekends, but I think the seeds of my scooter interest were born in my last year at school. One of my teachers rode a Swallow Gadabout Scooter; I believe it was made by the Swallow Coach Building Company (1935) Limited. Who would have thought that the original Lambretta Concessionaires Limited were only two miles from my home at 64 High Street, Epsom, Surrey.

My involvement in scooters has brought me many friends, far too many to name. They are all part of my memories and will stay with me for the rest of my life.

A special mention to all the people I have met at different workplaces and competitions through the years via Lambretta Club Great Britain, London Area Scooter Clubs Association and East Midland Scooter Clubs Association, also club members from abroad and The Scooter and Scooterist Magazine produced by Norrie Kerr, who was an active scooter racer. Norrie and I are still friends.

The most important person I met in the time since starting

out in Scootering, way back in 1956, was a young lady called Jan who had a new Red LI 150 Series I Lambretta, and she later became my wife. She has been the light of my life, as we have been through quite a few tough times together over the years, but the light still shines brightly!

It has often been said: 'if you remember the Sixties, you were not there', to that I say rubbish! It was a very special time for me and I would say for many other scooter addicts alike. Owning a scooter and going where you liked, when you liked, and meeting other people was fantastic. Riding a Lambretta became a way of life and, in those days, jobs were easy to come by. The Fifties and Sixties' music was brilliant. These are some of the reasons I have put pen to paper: to have a record to look back on, and also put right some of the things said about Lambretta Scooters that were not quite true.

Things did go wrong from time to time, but they were always put right to better the product for the benefit of the customer. One of the advertisements said, 'There is none better than a Lambretta'. One example was the London to Milan non-stop run in a time of seventeen odd hours.

Looking back over the years, I believe we have lived through the best of times. It was the age when if you were in trouble, people would stop and help if they could.

Special thanks must go to my wife Jan who has put up with me and my scooters for over sixty years and John Wood, who over all these years has kept in touch and helped Jan and I with the re-unions past and present of the Epsom Whirlwinds Lambretta Club.

CHAPTER 1
START OF A FANTASTIC LONG JOURNEY

Having left school in November 1954 at the tender age of fifteen, I was accepted by G & R Garages and Pump Engineers, as a motor mechanic apprentice on a six month trial. My new boss had requested a trial period as he did not think I would be able to travel the twelve miles by bike from my home in Epsom to Surbiton during the winter months. To me, it was a walk in the park as I was always out riding my bike.

Within a few months, I traded in my old bike for a brand-new Daws Tartan, five-star, ten-speed bicycle, my first pride and joy. During my second year of apprenticeship, the company took on selling Lambretta scooters. I had just passed my car driving test, and petrol rationing was introduced due to the Suez Crisis. This triggered a big increase in scooter sales, so a mechanic was needed to look after them.

No! Not me at this time. A lad that had been with the company for about six months was asked to look after them; unfortunately, he was not really up to the task of working on Lambretta scooters and, therefore, left soon after. I was then called to the office to see the boss. Well, I thought that was it; my time was up as well. Instead, I was asked if I would do the job; in return, my wages would be increased by sixpence an hour, plus a bonus on any accessories I sold. I was sent to Lambretta Concessionaires Limited at Wimbledon, Surrey to be trained, have my own workshop and all the tools needed to do the job. I would also be my own boss, much to the dismay of my foreman. Naturally, I said yes. I never got on with the foreman after that.

On returning to G & R's, from training at Lambretta Concessionaires Limited, the workshop had been completed and we were looking forward to the day when the ramp and tools arrived.

I was also told adverts were put in the local newspapers. Scooter Specialist, all makes repaired and serviced, also lawn mowers. He must have seen the look on my face and said, "You will manage — you will be fine."

Me, a specialist, after one week's training! By now, I was really interested in Lambretta Scooters and wanted one myself so I definitely would manage okay!

I told my boss I would like to buy a Lambretta. He explained he would work out all the details and let me know. Thirty pounds deposit was needed and the rest in instalments over two years.

I went home that night full of joy, Mum said, "OK, but you will have to find the deposit." What a blow, I only had about £5 0s 0d/£6 0s 0d in my savings account. Next day, I told the boss I would have to wait some time as I did not have the deposit. I was not feeling so happy now.

The next day, he told me I could have the Lambretta. He would pay the deposit for me and I would have to pay it back in my repayments. I would also have to wear a crash helmet and gloves, plus a windscreen had to be fitted and only one seat until I passed my test, which I did a few weeks later.

I dashed down to the showroom, picked out the scooter I liked, and filled in the forms for road tax, registration and insurance. I then had number plates made up and spent the rest of the day getting the machine ready for the road and went home on the scooter that night. By the time I returned to work the next day, I had done about 60 miles! Well, I obviously had to show it off to everyone I knew, not forgetting petrol was still on ration. Luckily, the garage had plenty of petrol when it went on ration, so I was OK if I needed the odd extra gallon or two.

My new pride and joy, no not the girl that is Ann from the office with other members of staff. They all came to see my new Lambretta Scooter, dark blue 1957 LDB 150 mark 2½, Registration Number 912CPJ — Price £164 0s 0d, plus the cost of accessories, road tax, insurance and number plates.

G&R's newly fitted out Lambretta Workshop.

It was at this point in time when I first met Rex White, who was then the technical representative. He had to inspect our workshop to make sure it was up to the standard for Lambretta workshop servicing, repairs and painted in the correct colours mid blue and white.

Courtesy of Mrs Edna Calder — Director — Lambretta Concessionaires.

The work bench had to be in place, all the tools had to be on a board on the wall, and the ramp set down so you could work all around the scooter with ease. Also, you had to have parts books and workshop manuals. The accessory catalogues were most important as that was where you made most of your money. Now I was all set to go. My thoughts turned to getting as much work as possible.

Listed below is the basic Tool Layout for a Lambretta Workshop 1954 onwards.

1. Cylinder-head spanner (125 c.c.).
2. Cylinder-head spanner (150 c.c.).
3. 8 mm handled socket spanner (for footboards, carburettor and general use).
4. Rear-hub extractor.
5. 19 mm socket for flywheel.
6. 19 mm socket (as above) with bar.
7. Flywheel holder.
8. Flywheel extractor.
9. Set of open-ended metric spanners (sizes 7, 8, 9, 10, 12, 14, 17, 19, 21, 24 and 27 mm).
10. Small Allen key 3·5 mm (for detachable cable nipples).
11. Small Allen key 4·5 mm (for headlamp and horn).
12. Small Allen key 5 mm (for clutch, transmission and kick-starter cases).
13. Small Allen key 6 mm (for transmission case).
14. Tank-neck spanner (125 c.c.).
15. Tank-neck spanner (150 c.c.).
16. Silencer-neck spanner.
17. Oil-plug tool
18. 27 mm spanner (for rear-wheel nut).
19. Clutch compressor.
20. Circlip pliers (contracting).
21. Circlip pliers (expanding).
22. Small-end bush extractor (14 mm).
23. Small-end bush extractor (16 mm).

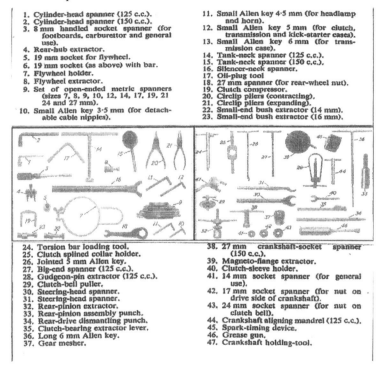

24. Torsion bar loading tool.
25. Clutch splined collar holder.
26. Jointed 5 mm Allen key.
27. Big-end spanner (125 c.c.).
28. Gudgeon-pin extractor (125 c.c.).
29. Clutch-bell puller.
30. Steering-head spanner.
31. Steering-head spanner.
32. Rear-pinion extractor.
33. Rear-pinion assembly punch.
34. Rear-drive dismantling punch.
35. Clutch-bearing extractor lever.
36. Long 6 mm Allen key.
37. Gear mesher.
38. 27 mm crankshaft-socket spanner (150 c.c.).
39. Magneto-flange extractor.
40. Clutch-sleeve holder.
41. 14 mm socket spanner (for general use).
42. 17 mm socket spanner (for nut on drive side of crankshaft).
43. 24 mm socket spanner (for nut on clutch bell).
44. Crankshaft aligning mandrel (125 c.c.).
45. Spark-timing device.
46. Grease gun.
47. Crankshaft holding-tool.

Courtesy of Mrs Edna Calder — Director of Lambretta Concessionaires.

Below are just a few examples of the prices for Lambretta Spares, from 1954 onwards, plus some of the cost of setting up a workshop. A ramp would have been £58 0s 0d and tools would have been around about the same price. A work bench with a vice was about £20 0s 0d. Painting the workshop in

Lambretta colours, inside and outside and painting the floor £30 0s 0d. Spares books, workshop instruction manuals and accessory catalogues around about £1 0s 0d each. This all seemed a lot of money to me at the time as I was only earning about £6 0s 0d a week!

Headlight Bulb	11s 0d
Saddle	£5 4s 0d
Electric Starter Motor	£28 4s 3d
Crankshaft	£6 15s 3d
Cylinder	£8 9s 0d
Piston	£1 6s 0d
Kick-start Pedal	£1 6s 0d
Tyre	£4 15s 9d
Tube	£1 3s 0d
Complete Front Brake Cable	£5s 6d
Rear Brake Cable	£5s 6d
Clutch cable with Adjuster	£9s 6d
Telex complete Gear Cable	£5 5s 11d
6 volt Battery for electric Starter	£6 2s 0d

Lambretta Concessionaires Stores and Service Department were located at 221/227 The Broadway, Wimbledon. SW19. The Guarantee Department and all technical and spares updates came from the Head Office at 424/426 Kingston Road, Rayne's Park, SW20.

A Lambretta Scooter hire Service was available for a short period of time but was closed as it was not profitable as some people just ran out of petrol and phoned in to say they had broken down! The showroom and office were then used by an ever expanding Spares Department.

G & R Garage, Surbiton, Surrey — 1956

This car was an Austin Healy 3000, beyond repair and is an example of the type of work I was doing before moving on to Lambretta Scooter repairs and servicing.

Filling new batteries with acid ready to fit on sold Lambretta machines.

As a Lambretta dealer, you could purchase these boxes with all the parts needed to service any LDB carburettor, and later on the LI and TV models.

Purchasing this box would have been at a special price and was well worth the expense, and could be topped up with parts as needed. The cost of the complete box would have been at least £20 0s 0d. A complete carburettor back in 1954 would have cost £5 11s 10d.

My Lambretta was now about two weeks old. I was in the front garden polishing my scooter before going out for a ride, when a lady came up to me to enquire about the scooter, as her son was interested in purchasing one. She lived further along the road, so I was up there like a shot. This would be my first sale and how I first met Peter Clarke. We became good friends. His Lambretta was a grey Mark II LDB 150, registration number: 316DPJ.

All lined up ready for servicing and repairs, including the Vespa. They all had full size windscreens which was one accessory that served you well in the winter months.

Peter and I showing off our new Lambretta Scooters. It was not a very nice day; later on, the fog came down and we lost our way home. This was our first Sunday run-out to Aldermaston in Hampshire where Peter's aunt and uncle lived and worked.

Peter's scooter was a Mark II and mine a Mark 2½ Early Mark III. We are back again at Aldermaston, Hampshire, with better weather and Peter's two young cousins are on the back of our scooters.

Easter was drawing nearer and we decided to go camping in Devon. Peter took a mate from work and I took my brother Mervyn. My aunt and uncle lived in Teignmouth, Devon; good enough reason to go there for our holiday and show off our new scooters.

Friday came at last — no more work for a few days — two fully laden scooters and four lads started off to Devon. It took nine hours of hard riding (172 miles) (276.807 kilometres) to get to Dawlish, Devon where we found a good camp site right by the main road.

The weather for the long weekend was good for the time of year. We were out and about every day, up on the Moors and all around the coast, not to mention around my Aunt's a few times for a free snack. We also met a lot of people including a few girls! All too quickly the Easter weekend was over.

Two German girls who were touring Devon and Cornwall that we met at the camp site.

It was time to pack up, say our goodbyes to a family we had met at the camp site and start our journey home at 9.30 a.m. arriving home at 7.30 p.m., after a long stop for lunch, as the weather was good; which did not give us too much time to get ready for work the next day.

Our favourite coffee shop in Dawlish, Devon. We were regular visitors.

As soon as Peter got his scooter and before our planned holiday, we decided to start up a club and set about letting everybody we knew what we were planning. So it was no surprise when we got home, my mum said that three lads had called around asking about getting scooters and joining the club. This meant more sales for me.

We all met around my house as soon as they got their scooters. The name we decided on for our club was 'The Vikings' and the badge we used was from the Rover 90 car as I worked in the garage. I still have my badge today. We found a hall to hold our Wednesday evening meetings, which was the old Cricketers Pub, West Hill, Epsom, Surrey.

Our meeting place for Sunday runs was at the Clock Tower in Epsom, Surrey. We would go to the coast on a good day. If not we would go to London Zoo, Beaulieu Museum, Kew Gardens, Blue Bell Railway in Sussex, Windsor Castle and Longleat Safari Park to name just a few places.

The Mark 2½ is the model I purchased and rode for two years.

Listed below are the parts that differ from the Mark III:
Kick start Pedal
Kick start Rubber (grey)
Silencer
Air filter
Chrome support on top of frame
Chrome handlebars
Light switch
Grey sleeving on cables
Leg shield and badge
Horn casting and headlamp rim
Army grey/green seat covers
Front leg shields glove box
Flywheel
Grease nipples
Chrome wheel nuts
Chrome wheel spindle nuts

Front brake plate
Front brake cam and lever
Rear hub
Rear hub nut and locking bolt
Speedo and cable
No grease nipple on kick-start body

Mark 2½ parts that differ from Mark II:
Frame
Rear light
Colour blue not grey
Main engine casing
Complete kick start unit
Silencer
Longer gear cables
Longer rear brake cable

At least 600 of these information sheets were supplied for all
D, LD, LI Series I, Series II, and TV Series I.

Most Dealers had these Technical and Modification folders which kept
mechanics up to date with all the latest modifications. I always wrote
mine straight into the parts book as this would save a lot of time when
ordering spare parts.

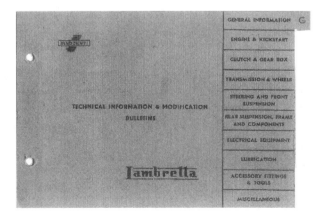

All the bulletins sent to Dealers were kept in the right section as
you can see above, which kept everything tidy and easy to find.

This is a sample of what was sent to workshops, I have hundreds of these sheets which included the Three Wheeler machines as well. These gave the Engine Number that the new part started from. When a Lambretta came in for repair the mechanic knew which parts to order.

WORKING AT G & R'S GARAGE

My Boss had a nephew who lived and worked in London. He had a Bella 200, but was unhappy with the dealer he purchased it from so he came to our Workshop for service and repairs.

This was great as I got to drive the works van. When the Bella was in for repair, I would take the van home that night and set off very early the next morning for Ambassador Motorcycles Ltd., Pontiac works, Fern Bank Road, Ascot, Berkshire, to get there when it opened.

Apart from the Bella scooters, they also sold NSU Motorcycles; they had a twin 2 stroke 250cc engine and were fast. The main trouble I had with Bella scooters was the ignition switch. They over-heated causing damage to the wires and batteries if not detected straight away. Damp and rain was the problem, no WD40 in those days! Other troubles I had with the Bella were plugs oiling up and silencer needing a clean out. This applied to all scooters at that time, not much Two Stroke oil about then; SAE 30 Oil was used at about 1/2 pint to the gallon.

About 90% of my work was on Lambretta machines

which also included quite a few NSU Scooters. NSU had the same problem with ignition switches, with hind sight a few of the scooters may have been left uncovered in the rain. This time it meant me going up to London for parts to NSU Concessionaires GB Limited, 7 Chesterfield Gardens, London later the company moved to 136 King Street, London W6.

I also worked on Moto Rumi, I really liked them, so much so I almost bought one. As luck would have it, my long time mate Mick brought a Moto Rumi just before going on holiday to Devon, with his girlfriend Margaret. The machine had a terrible time getting up the hills. On his return from holiday, he traded it in for another Lambretta. So I stayed with my Lambretta which proved to be much better on longer runs for two up riding.

Motor Rumi Concessionaires at this time were at 149 High Street, Harlesden, NW10.

Our club went to Brands Hatch to watch Motorcycle Racing and were surprised to see a Moto Rumi racing in the 125cc class. The machine was quick on acceleration, but lost out on the hills through lack of power at lower revs. The racing was most enjoyable.

I also worked on Vespa Scooters and brought all the spares from Kingston Scooters. This is where I first met George Savage and his wife. It would be some years later that I would be working for them, after completing my National Service.

There were many other makes of scooters I worked on BSA, Capri, ISO, Piatti to name but a few. Other makes of scooters I took a shine to, were the TWN Contessa, DKR Capella and Diana. I was put off the Diana on a club run to Brighton. We were riding along the seafront and spotted a café. As we pulled up and parked a 59 Club member came out of the café, saw the look on our faces and said, it is alright come on in; by the way one of your scooters is on fire. Yeah, haven't we heard that one before? Luckily we did look back to find the Diana was on fire and was distinguished from water in the gutter. What luck it was pouring with rain, you do not often say that. It took about fifteen minutes repairing the wires with insulation tape. We were very cold and wet with very dirty black hands so we decided to go back home.

Another club member had a Triumph 250 Tigress and always wore a long coat on his scooter. We found out it was because the top of the engine was very close to the seat, which made it very warm. This was not so good on a summer's day. The scooter was quite good looking, apart from the motorcycle rear lamp which was just stuck on the back. The acceleration and brakes were very good. We also had Peugeot and Capri scooters as well as other makes, all at different times, which helped to make a really good Scooter Club.

My mates and I had a second holiday in Dawlish, Devon with more scooters joining us at the same camp site. On the way down, Peter Ward on his LDB 150 broke a clutch cable. No panic, I was carrying all cables, bulbs and plugs. When I opened the box with the clutch cable in it, there was no inner cable, just the outer. To fix this, we had to wind the old clutch inner cable round the rear brake pedal, so when he pushed the pedal down for the brake it pulled the clutch lever on the engine at the same time. We made it into Exeter like that and found a dealer to buy a cable. No more troubles after that and once again we had a great holiday. The weather had been good, but I was looking forward to getting home and a soft bed.

My mates and me on the far right on our second holiday. Peter took the photo.

It was back to work once more and there were plenty of scooters waiting for me to repair. The garage ran a 24 hour breakdown service for the AA and RAC so I used to get quite a lot of accident work. One of the accident jobs was a 48cc Lambretta moped with a bent pedal arm, bent forks and damage to the paintwork and front mudguard; not a big job! On the road test after repair, I found the front brake very poor for the speed this moped could do. A quick service on the brake and road tested again. It was better, but not as good as I would have liked. The suspension front and back was good and with 2 speeds it was a good moped to ride.

The LDA Mark III Electric start model for some reason suffered with a poor rear brake. The problem was overcome, up to a point, by fitting a softer rear lining made by NU-TEXA, from Fuller Frictions Ltd, Bristol. These came as a boxed pair with rivets to secure them to the aluminium shoes; they were also very resistant to oil penetration. The problem may have been the rear hub, brake cam or the peg the shoes were located on. I only came across this problem on the LDA; so I put it down to the engine being on a different production line to the kick start engines.

The FD 150 Three Wheeler was a very popular commercial vehicle and mainly used in parks and golf courses, because of its lightweight. It did little damage to the ground when picking up grass cuttings and compost. The best bit was the fun you could have riding them about on the grass. Almost 30,000 FD and FDC machines were produced from 1955/1959.

LAMBRETTA MOPED BROCHURE PLUS 3 WHEELER BROCHURE

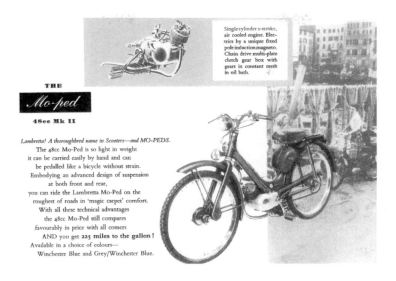

Single cylinder 2-stroke, air cooled engine. Electrics by a unique fixed pole induction magneto. Chain drive multi-plate clutch gear box with gears in constant mesh in oil bath.

THE

Mo-ped

48cc Mk II

Lambretta! A thoroughbred name in Scooters—and MO-PEDS.
The 48cc Mo-Ped is so light in weight it can be carried easily by hand and can be pedalled like a bicycle without strain. Embodying an advanced design of suspension at both front and rear, you can ride the Lambretta Mo-Ped on the roughest of roads in 'magic carpet' comfort. With all these technical advantages the 48cc Mo-Ped still compares favourably in price with all comers AND you get **225 miles to the gallon !** Available in a choice of colours— Winchester Blue and Grey/Winchester Blue.

SPECIFICATIONS

150 cc MODELS

Engine	Single Cylinder two-stroke
Capacity	148 cc
Compression Ratio	6:1
Tank Capacity	2¼ galls.
Speed	50/55 m.p.h
Consumption	100/130 m.p.g
Mixture	½ pt. oil to 1 gall.
Wheelbase	50¼"
Length overall	70"
Weight	198 lbs.

125 cc MODELS

Engine	Single Cylinder two-stroke
Capacity	123 cc
Compression Ratio	6:1
Tank Capacity	1¾ galls.
Speed	45/50 m.p.h
Consumption	130 m.p.g.
Mixture	½ pt. oil to 1 gall.
Wheelbase	50¼"
Length overall	70"
Weight	194 lbs.

48 cc MO-PED

Engine	Single cylinder two-stroke
Capacity	48 cc
Compression Ratio	Power 1.7 h.p.
Tank Capacity	4½ pints
Speed	30/35 m.p.h.
Consumption	225 m.p.g.
Mixture	½ pt. oil to 1 gall.
Wheelbase	46¾"
Length overall	74¼"
Weight	97 lbs.

WHY YOU SHOULD BUY

Lambretta

Here are five salient points for you to compare :

PRICE — Lambretta have models to suit all pockets. From the £71 Mo-Ped to the £197 Mayfair, you can be assured of value and quality for your money.

POPULARITY — Lambretta are the most popular make. Count them on the road today!

EXPERIENCE — Lambretta are mechanically more reliable. As one of the pioneers of the motor scooter, Lambretta are renowned for mechanical superiority and trouble-free scootering.

AFTER-SALES SERVICE — Lambretta have the finest after-sales service in the country. There is a network of over 1,000 dealers to give you speedy service in maintenance and spares — as described overleaf.

ORGANISATION — Lambretta Concessionaires Ltd. — an established name. One of the oldest and largest scooter firms in Great Britain and an all-British enterprise.

FOR FURTHER DETAILS AND DEMONSTRATION SEE YOUR LOCAL DEALER TODAY

Courtesy of Mrs. Edna Calder — Director of Lambretta Concessionaires.

The photo right showing the NU-TEXA brake linings to fit on front and rear shoes for LDB scooters. Other manufacturers also made brake linings to fit on the LI series.

BELLA 200

The Bella was a big robust scooter. It weighed in at 322lb (146kg) and the saddle height was 2ft 6 inches (76.0cm). It was a single cylinder two-stroke with a power output of 12 BHP at 5.400 RPM, a 12 volt electrical start system, 4 speed foot operated gear change, 3.50 x 12 tyres on good solid aluminium wheels, hydraulic shock absorbers front and rear with good brakes.

The rear heel operated brake pedal was on the left-hand side of the scooter. The foot operated gear change was on the right-hand side of the scooter which took a bit of getting used too after riding Lambretta and Vespa Scooters.

Courtesy of Brian Cook.

The engine was air flow cooled, not fan assisted, so it had a large cylinder head to take away the heat. These cylinder heads were modified and used on the Don Noy's Stingray Scramble Scooters, back in 1959/1960.

A centre stand was fitted as standard as well as a side stand. I liked the fold away rear footrest and the luggage hook

26

on the leg shield, also the handlebar mirror was like the one that could be used on the LDB Lambretta Scooters.

Along with repairing scooters, I had the use of the van to repair lawn mowers in the Surbiton and Esher, Surrey areas and most of the time it was just an oiled up plug or dirty carburettor. Once or twice, they had just run out of petrol! I would find their empty petrol can and get some petrol and make sure the mower ran OK. Then, I'd wait weeks to be paid for the work.

Another job was at a riding stable. A young girl had a NSU moped that was always going wrong. I often wondered if she and her friends deliberately messed about with the machine, just so they could all stand around giggling while I sorted it out. I used to hate going there because it was a waste of time and money. I cannot print what I said under my breath each time I left.

The coldest place I ever worked was in a hospital mortuary. The man was unable to hold any tools because, in his line of work, performing autopsies, he had damaged most of the tops of his fingers.

He had an old 1954 D model. The taper on the flywheel and crank had completely gone because he had been unable to tighten the flywheel nut up enough because of his hands. I advised the owner on the cost of repairs, but it was too

Christine Jackson's D model Lambretta very similar to the scooter mentioned above. Courtesy of Christine Jackson.

expensive. I never found out what happened to the scooter. As I have tried numerous times to get information to print this advertisement, please contact me if there are any queries.

SCOOTER WORLD

FEBRUARY, 1957   NINEPENCE

A scooter, snow — and ski

THE MOTOR SCOOTER MAGAZINE

● Home and Away ● On Minor Roads ● Upon Reflection ● Scooter Accessories ● Lambretta Electrics ● Two-Stroke Topics (iv)—Oils and Greases ● Youth Hostels Again ● From Your Clubs

This was the best magazine for the Scooterist at the time. It showed many adverts for accessories, cloths, helmets, technical information, advice, scooter club news, plus letters from around the country and much more.

28

OUR OWN CLUB MAGAZINE

Epsom Whirlwinds Lambretta Club also printed a monthly Club Magazine. It contained reports on club activities, technical advice, results of events and names of new members.

In the early days of the LD and D models all the gear, clutch, throttle and front brake cables came complete as they had soldered nipples both ends. By the time the Mark 2½ and Mark III were on sale you could buy inner cables which made life a lot easier for the dealer, and the customer's pocket. The inner cables could be fitted to earlier models as well with solder less nipples.

An exchange engine could be purchased in those days, but it had to be 125 for 125, Mark I for Mark I. An exchange engine had a different engine number. The same applied when exchanging frames after an accident, which should be entered into your log book. It was possible to purchase all frames, panels, leg shields and mudguards sprayed in the right colours, which meant a quick turnaround to get the scooter back on the road.

On the service side of things, these were carried out at 500, 1,500 and 3,000 miles. Most customers just went for the 3,000 service when the engine and frame was completely washed down. Gearbox oil and axle oil changed. The fly wheel removed, contacts cleaned, check coils and re-time engine, clean the plug, carburettor and filter. Remove wheels and hubs, clean brake shoes and hubs, grease the cams, refit front wheel to the back hub and fit the back wheel to the front hub. This was done to even-out the tyre wear. Adjust tyre pressures; check all cables, fit new if required. Check all lights, horn and battery, wheel and steering bearings. Grease all nipples, especially the one on the torsion bar. You needed to make sure the grease came out past the rubber protection band, to stop water going in the torsion bar. The centre stand pin that runs through the frame, needed to be kept well oiled, if not it would seize up. On my scooter, I drilled two holes in the frame tube so I could oil it better.

Another little trick to help get the rear wheel off with ease, (as some tyres had a very heavy tread pattern on them), was to cut a small piece off the inside lug that the panel catch was located on. Later we would do the same on the LI/TV I and II Lambrettas.

SUMMER HOLIDAY IN DEVON

This is a photo of my Aunt Marge and Uncle Sid
sitting on my scooter outside their home in
Teignmouth, Devon.

This was our camp site in Starcross, near Dawlish, Devon and a family
we met. We met a couple of girls on the camp site. They were doing
our washing up for us, in return for a ride on our scooters.

Another family we met at the camp site that came from Doncaster
towing a caravan. It took them two days to get to Devon and two days
back home again.

Lambretta 150cc D 55

£108 : 4 : 7 plus £21 : 12 : 11 P.Tax
P/SEAT (optional) EXTRA

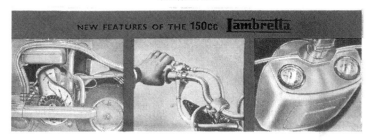

NEW FEATURES OF THE 150cc **Lambretta**

IMPROVED COOLING:

Engine cooling has been improved on the new models by adopting the forced draught system. This has previously been exclusive to the LD model, but now both models are assured of efficient cooling under any climatic conditions.

BETTER GEAR CHANGING:

The new method adopted for the engagement of gears ensures instantaneous and perfect engagement. Gear changing is made easier for the novice by the double flexible cable and the audible click which occurs when engaging gear.

IMPROVED INSTRUMENT PANEL:

The front legshield of the LD model now has a metal pocket for documents, gloves and other incidentals. This also serves as a mounting for the speedometer and the clock and is yet another sign that Lambretta owners are offered the same facilities as those given to car owners.

Courtesy of Mrs. Edna Calder — Director of Lambretta
Concessionaires.

The LDB 150 was about £16 0s 0d extra to purchase than the D model, but outsold it by far in the UK because of the better weather protection.

A photograph of a very young Dick Sedgley on holiday in Devon.

Yes, that is me showing off my new scooter with its many accessories, which are as listed. Double leg shield saver boarders — footboard extensions — side panel air scoops — rear extension carrier — handlebar mirror — badge bar — windscreen, plus the front mudguard bumper, which I liked most of all. I wish I had one for my scooter today. Peter's scooter is in the background.

Courtesy of Mrs. Edna Calder — Director of Lambretta
Concessionaires.
TOP OF THE RANGE MODEL LDA AND LDB LAMBRETTA
BROCHURE

The very last LDB Mark III I sold was an all red Mayfair model to a lady. When she asked about the Lambretta I thought it was for her daughter/son but in fact it was for her. Listed are the accessories she wanted, Benzi windscreen, double leg shields saver boarders, front bumper, saddle and wheel covers, floor mat, two handlebar mirrors, front fork suspension box covers in aluminium with red paint, a complete scooter cover and a complete kick start fitted. The biggest surprise of all was the Abarth sport silencer with twin chrome pipes. The profit on all these accessories was much more than the profit on the scooter, which was great news for me as I was paid a bonus on accessories sales. That is why I remember this particular sale so well.

SOUTH DOWNS IN SUSSEX

Hill Climb event and some Epsom Scooter Club members at the top of the course overlooking the finish line.

Photo of our club badge we had made to fit on a badge bar for our scooters.

During 1958/59, the Epsom Scooter Club grew in strength and many new friends were gained during this period. Scooters were now very popular and things at work were going really well. By this time, I knew I had to do two years National Service for my queen and country. G & R had to find someone to train to do my job for two years whilst I was away.

Peter Clarke and I were riding around Epsom town centre when a friend waved to us, it was Roy Walton, he was going out with a girl whose sister and friend had scooters. We were round Lynn's house like a shot. Jan, (my future wife) had an LI 150 Series I Lambretta in red/white, registration number: 224JPL and Lynn had a TV 175 Series I Lambretta, cream in colour, registration number: 192GPG. Peter and I had also purchased a TV 175 Series I Lambretta; Peter's was in cream, registration number: 478JPC and mine was coffee/cream, registration number: 144JPC. After much talking and looking at the scooters, the two girls decided to join the scooter club. Up to now we had been just a social club, going out on a Sunday enjoying ourselves riding our scooters. It was Jan, the new girl, who asked why the club had not joined the British Lambretta Owners Association (BLOA). As soon as we could, our scooter club joined.

It was at this point we found out there already was a club called The Vikings. It appeared that some of our members did not like the name Vikings, so a new name had to be found. There was much debating and eventually, Epsom Whirlwinds

Scooter Club was decided upon. We also decided to have banners made for the leg shields. They were handmade in material of red or yellow, with black embroidered lettering and tapes attached to tie around the leg shields. They were mainly made by Jan's mum and my Aunt May. Some members may have embroidered their own banner. I believe we were the only club to make our own banners and badges.

Our scooter club banners and home-made badges for our jackets.

Our clubs' metal Viking badge before we changed the name to Whirlwinds.

My BLOA badge from the sixties.

Latest modified parts for mark 2 ½ and Mark III. These parts were only used on a small number of scooters. My LDB 150 Mark 2 ½ were fitted with these parts.

SPARE PARTS 125/150 LD

Fig. No.	Part No.	Description	Quantity
1 {	12181356	Frame with bush at fig. 2 (150 LD)	1
	12181451	Frame with bush at fig. 2 (125 LD)	1
2	07180160	Bush, torsion bar support	1
3	12181366	Lid for luggage box with lock and keys, fig. 4	1
4	12181371	Lock and key (fig. 5) for luggage box	1
5	12180249	Keys	2
6	12180234	Pin, luggage box hinge	1
7	12180225	Spring, luggage box lid	1
8	12180226	Retainer for spring	1
9	12180223	Tube, spring guide	1
10	12180228	Beading, luggage box lid	1
11	12180348	Clip for holding tool kit	1
12	12180244	Hook, lid spring	1
13	03180109	Rubber grommet	2
14	70850406	Screw, battery earth wire (150 LD)	1
15	73170043	Washer, spring (150 LD)	1
16	70880430	Screw, battery holder (150 LD)	1
17	11010560	Trunnion, battery holder (150 LD)	1
18	11010559	Threaded trunnion, battery holder (150 LD)	1
19	07180616	Rubber buffer	1
20	12181061	Buffer, for side panel	2
21	73000003	Nut, for fixing buffer	2
22	12180237	Insulating plate, luggage box	2
23	12180238	Insulating strip, luggage box	2
24	70360518	Screw for fixing plate and strip	4
25	73170053	Washer, spring, for fig. 24	4
26	73060053	Washer, plain, for fig. 24	4
27	12111191	Cowl, rear upper engine	1
28	12110518	Plate for fixing cowl	1
29	12110520	« U » bolt	1
30	72000005	Nut for figs. 29 and 54	3
31	73170053	Washer, spring, for figs. 30, 51, 60	12
32	12161558	Panel, right hand	1
33	12180269	Grill for panel	2
34	12090368	Lock, right hand panel, compl. with fig. 36, 38, 39, 40, 42, 43, 44, 45	1
35	12090367	Lock, left hand panel, compl. with fig. 37 to 45	1

VI

Right hand photo showing part numbers 22 to 31.

Top left of bottom photo rear upper engine cowl with fixing brackets.
Bottom right of photo luggage box insulation strip with fixings.

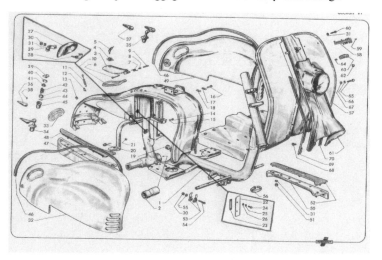

CHAPTER 2
LAMBRETTA ACCESSORIES AND IMPROVEMENTS

Photograph of Mr PJ Agg sent to me by Mrs Edna Calder — Director
of Lambretta Concessionaires to put in book.

Mr. P.J. Agg on a Mark II LDB 150 outside the Lambretta
Concessionaires Limited — Motor Scooter Accessory Shop
424-426 Kingston Road, SW20.

The Service Department was situated on the Broadway and the Hire Shop on the opposite side of the road would become the Spares Department.

After the sad loss of P.J. Agg, I was asked by Colin Rowlinson founder and chairman of the GT 200 Club, and Peter Pooley events and admissions secretary, if I would take up the position of honorary president, which I was most happy to do.

lambretta

COMPLETE RANGE OF ACCESSORIES

LAMBRETTA CONCESSIONAIRES STORES DEPARTMENT, 424/426 KINGSTON ROAD, RAYNES PARK, S.W.20.
Telephone : CHErrywood 3204 (5 lines)

All these accessories pages are courtesy of Mrs Edna Calder — Director of Lambretta Concessionaires.

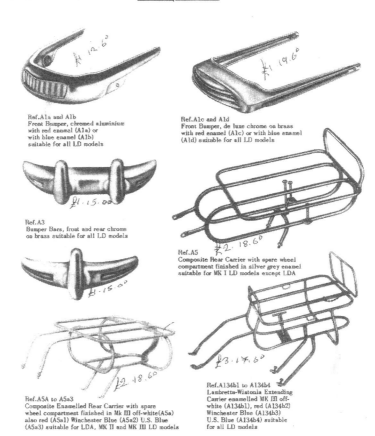

Ref.A1a and A1b
Front Bumper, chromed aluminium
with red enamel (A1a) or
with blue enamel (A1b)
suitable for all LD models

Ref.A1c and A1d
Front Bumper, de luxe chrome on brass
with red enamel (A1c) or with blue enamel
(A1d) suitable for all LD models

Ref.A3
Bumper Bars, front and rear chrome
on brass suitable for all LD models

Ref.A5
Composite Rear Carrier with spare wheel
compartment finished in silver grey enamel
suitable for MK I LD models except LDA

Ref.A5A to A5a3
Composite Enamelled Rear Carrier with spare
wheel compartment finished in Mk III off-white(A5a)
also red (A5a1) Winchester Blue (A5a2) U.S. Blue
(A5a3) suitable for LDA, MK II and MK III LD models

Ref.A134b1 to A134b4
Lambretta-Wistonia Extending
Carrier enamelled MK III off-
white (A134b1), red (A134b2)
Winchester Blue (A134b3)
U.S. Blue (A134b4) suitable
for all LD models

42

7.60

Ref.A21
Exhaust Deflector chrome on
brass suitable for MK 1
machines and MK III LD fitted
with long silencer tube

Ref.A23
Horn Cover, large chrome
on brass suitable for
MK I and MK II LD models

7.60

Ref.A25
Suspension Box Covers
chrome on brass suitable
for all D and LD models

8.60

Ref.A23a
Horn Cover, small chrome
on brass suitable for MK I
and MK II LD models

7.60

Ref. A25a and A25b
Suspension Box Covers,
de luxe chromed aluminium
with red enamel (A25a) or
with blue enamel (A25b)
suitable for all D and LD
models   *10.60*

Ref.A24
Horn Cover, superior
chrome on brass
suitable for MK I and
MK II LD models
15.00

Ref.A30   *£2.20.0*
Glove Box with speedo and clock
mount, grey only suitable for MK 1
LD125 and MK III models except
LDA
PRICE FOR THE CLOCK £3.1.0

Ref.A29
Speedometer mounting
with package hook for
LD125 MK 1
10.00

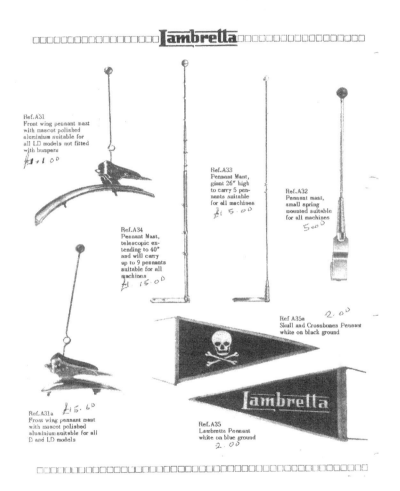

Ref.A31
Front wing pennant mast
with mascot polished
aluminium suitable for
all LD models not fitted
with bumpers
£1.10.0

Ref.A33
Pennant Mast,
giant 26" high
to carry 5 pen-
nants suitable
for all machines
£1.5.00

Ref.A32
Pennant mast,
small spring
mounted suitable
for all machines
5.00

Ref.A34
Pennant Mast,
telescopic ex-
tending to 40"
and will carry
up to 9 pennants
suitable for all
machines
£1.15.00

Ref A35a   2.00
Skull and Crossbones Pennant
white on black ground

Ref.A31a   £15.60
Front wing pennant mast
with mascot polished
aluminium suitable for all
D and LD models

Ref.A35
Lambretta Pennant
white on blue ground
2.00

Ref.A36   5.3⁰
Headlamp Hood, chrome on brass suitable
for all D and LD models

Ref.A36a and A36b
Headlamp Hood and Horn
Casing in chromed
aluminium with red
enamel (A36a) or with
blue enamel (A36b) suit-
able for MK I and MK II
LD models
£2.10.0⁰

Ref.A37 £1.15.0⁰
Saver Borders chrome on
brass suitable for all LD
models

Ref.A39a   12.0⁰
Side Panel Flashes chrome on brass with blue
line suitable for all LD models

Ref.A40   £1.5.0⁰
Stop light with number plate
bracket to fit rear mudguard
(supplied without switch and
bulbs) suitable for MK I LD
models

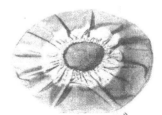

Ref.A52 to A52c   18.6⁰
Plastic Spare Wheel Cover grey (A52)
red tartan (A52a) blue tartan (A52b)
green tartan (A52c)

45

Ref.A43
Spare Wheel Mount finished
grey enamel for MK I LD150
(not suitable for LDA)

£1 . 0 . 0ᴰ

Ref.A46
(not illustrated)
Spare Wheel with white
wall tyre *£6 3 . 6ᴰ*

Ref.A43a *£1 . 10 . 0ᴰ*
Spare Wheel Mount in MK III
off-white enamel suitable for
MK II and MK III LD models
(not suitable for LDA)

£5 . 2 . 6ᴰ

Ref.A45 Spare
Wheel (black tyre)

Ref.A49 *£17. 9*
Spare Wheel Disc chrome
on brass for use only
with composite rear
carrier

Ref.A50 *19.6ᴰ*
Wheel Disc, chrome on brass,
suitable for fitment to rear wheel
or to spare wheel mounted on A43
bracket

Ref.A48 *£2 . 10 . 0ᴰ*
Chrome Wheel Rim suitable
for all LD and D models

Ref.A51 *£1 . 10 . 0ᴰ*
Wheel Disc with spokes chrome
on brass suitable for fitment to
rear wheel or to spare wheel
mounted on A43 bracket

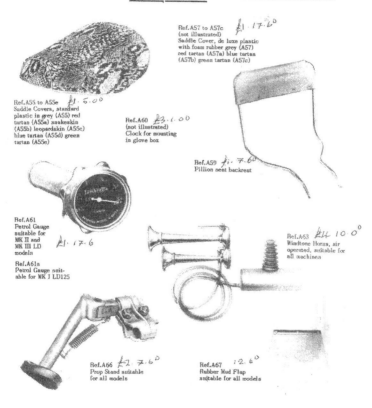

Ref.A57 to A57c
(not illustrated)
Saddle Cover, de luxe plastic
with foam rubber grey (A57)
red tartan (A57a) blue tartan
(A57b) green tartan (A57c)

£1. 17. 6

Ref.A55 to A55e   £1. 5. 0 0
Saddle Covers, standard
plastic in grey (A55) red
tartan (A55a) snakeskin
(A55b) leopardskin (A55c)
blue tartan (A55d) green
tartan (A55e)

Ref.A60   £3. 1. 0 0
(not illustrated)
Clock for mounting
in glove box

Ref.A59   £1. 7. 6
Pillion seat backrest

Ref.A61
Petrol Gauge
suitable for
MK II and
MK III LD
models

£1. 17. 6

Ref.A61a
Petrol Gauge suit-
able for MK I LD125

Ref.A63   £4. 10. 0
Windtone Horns, air
operated, suitable for
all machines

Ref.A66   £2. 7. 6
Prop Stand suitable
for all models

Ref.A67   12. 6
Rubber Mud Flap
suitable for all models

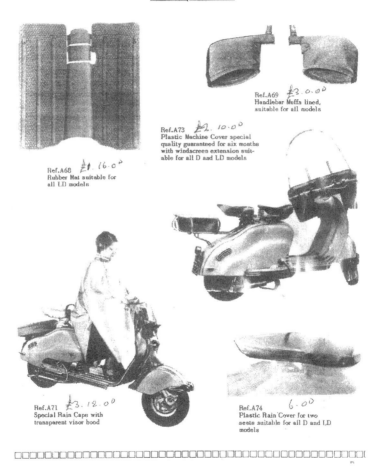

Ref.A69 £3.0.0.0
Handlebar Muffs lined,
suitable for all models

Ref.A73 £2.10.0.0
Plastic Machine Cover special
quality guaranteed for six months
with windscreen extension suitable for all D and LD models

Ref.A68 £1.16.0.0
Rubber Mat suitable for
all LD models

Ref.A71 £3.12.0.0
Special Rain Cape with
transparent visor hood

Ref.A74 6.0.0
Plastic Rain Cover for two
seats suitable for all D and LD
models

Ref.A90 to A90f   4.9ᴰ
Tipon Paint Pencil grey (A90),
red (A90a) Winchester Blue (A90b)
MK III off-white (A90f)

Ref.A100 and A100a
(not illustrated)
Lambretta Lapel Badge with
pin (A100) or with stud (A100a)

Ref.A99   4.6ᴰ
Keyring with leather
fob and enamelled badge

Ref.A107   £4·10·0ᴰ
Touring Case for Rear Carrier
grey plastic to match A75 and
A121 Pannier Bags

Ref.A91 to A91g   2·0ᴰ
(not illustrated) Touch-up Paint
¼ pint tin grey (A91), red (A91a)
Winchester Blue (A91b) off-white
(A91c) 48cc red (A91d) U.S. Blue
(A91e) MK III off-white (A91f)
slate blue (A91g)

Ref.A92 to A92f   6·0ᴰ
(not illustrated) Touch-up Paint
½ pint tin grey (A92), red (A92a)
Winchester Blue (A92b) off-white
(A92c) MK III off-white (A92f)

Ref.A93 to A93f   11·6ᴰ
(not illustrated) Touch-up Paint
1 pint tin grey (A93) off-white
(A93c) MK III off-white (A93f)

Ref.A95   £1·2·6ᴰ
(not illustrated) Hand Paint
Sprayer complete, grey only

Ref.A114   £1·10·00
Parking Light Kit suitable for
LD 150 MK I model

Ref.A115   £5·6·8ᴰ
Abarth super Silencer suitable
for all LD 150 machines and
LD 125 MK III

Ref.A.118A
(not illustrated) £1·4·9ᴰ
Grease gun suitable for all
machines fitted with
hydraulic nipples

Ref.A118
(not illustrated) £1·4·9ᴰ
'Nubrex' Lambretta Grease
Gun suitable for all machines
fitted with hexagonal nipples

Ref.A117 and A117a
Benzi SPORTS Windscreen
a lower windscreen for the
shorter rider and enthusiast,
grey only, suitable for all
MK I and MK II models also
A117a suitable for MK III
models £5·5·0ᴰ

Ref.A126 *£4.19.6*
Luggage Box Carrier similar to A110
carrier but with locked compartment
instead of petrol tank finished grey
enamel suitable for MK I LD models

Ref.A110 *£7.10.0*
Petrol Tank Carrier grey enamel finish
Petrol tank holds 1 gallon petrol and ½
pint oil suitable for MK I LD models

Ref.A11
Footboard Extensions, polished
aluminium suitable for all LD *£2.2.00*
models

£1.17.6

Ref.A15
Heelplates, standard polished
aluminium suitable for all LD
models

Ref.A128 and A128a *£2.5.0*
Heelplates, super chromed aluminium
with red enamel (A128) or with blue
enamel (A128a)

Ref.A16 *£4.7.6*
Heelplates, de luxe chrome
on brass suitable for all LD
models

Ref.A20 *£2.5.0*
Side Panel Grilles, de luxe
chrome on brass matching A16
heelplates suitable for all LD
models

Ref.A19 *10.6*
Side Panel Grilles chrome on brass
suitable for all LD models

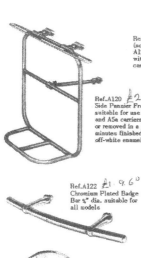

Ref.A120a £3.3.00
(not illustrated) As
A120 but for use
with A110 and A126
carriers

Ref.A120 £2.5.00
Side Pannier Frames
suitable for use with A5
and A5a carriers Fitted
or removed in a few
minutes finished in MK III
off-white enamel

Ref.A121
Grey Plastic Pannier Bag for A120 and A120a
frames. These bags lock onto the frames safe-
guarding contents when machine is left
unattended £2.12.6 (B20H)

Ref.A122 £1.9.6
Chromium Plated Badge
Bar ¾" dia. suitable for
all models

£1.12.6
Ref.A124
Steering Headlock for 48cc

Ref.A123 and A123a
Benzi Windscreen for
48cc complete with
red apron (A123) or
with grey apron (A123a)
£4.10.00

Ref.A125 £1.3.6
Mirror, fitting to legshield
suitable for all models

▯▯▯

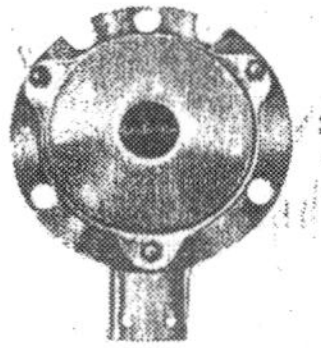

Ref. A43
Spare wheel bracket
for LD150
£1 6.8ᵈ

Ref. A41
(not illustrated)
Spare wheel bracket
for D
£1 · 5 · 8ᵈ

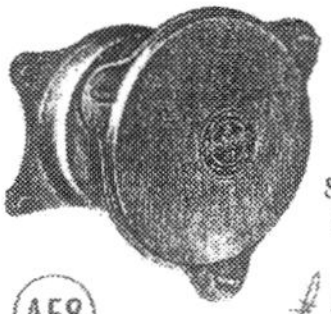

Ref. A42
Spare whee
bracket foi
LD125
£1 · 5 · 8ᵈ

A44

A58

A6

A26

A38

A45

A14

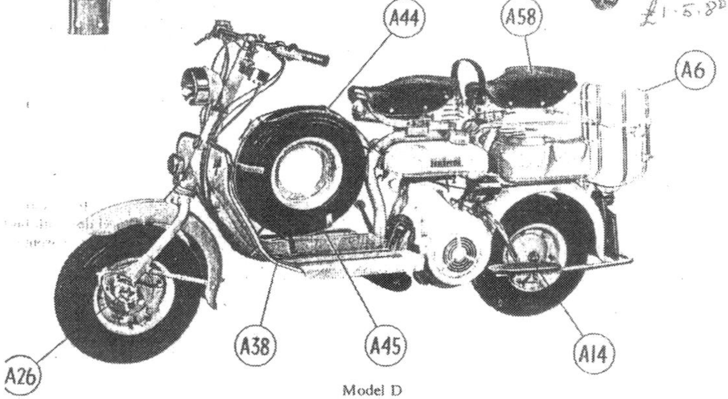

Model D
with accessories
attached

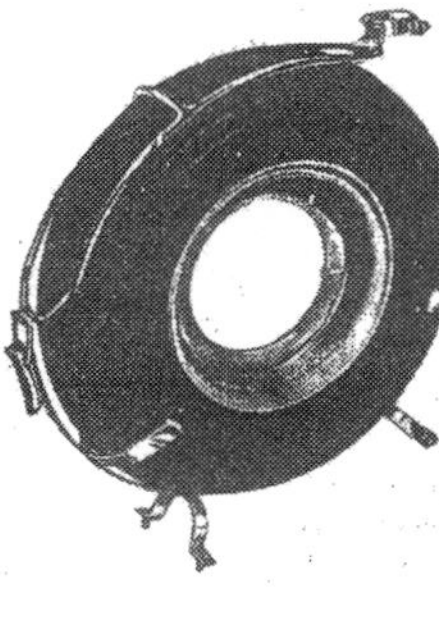

Ref. A44
Spare wheel carrier,
chrome, for D
£2 10.00

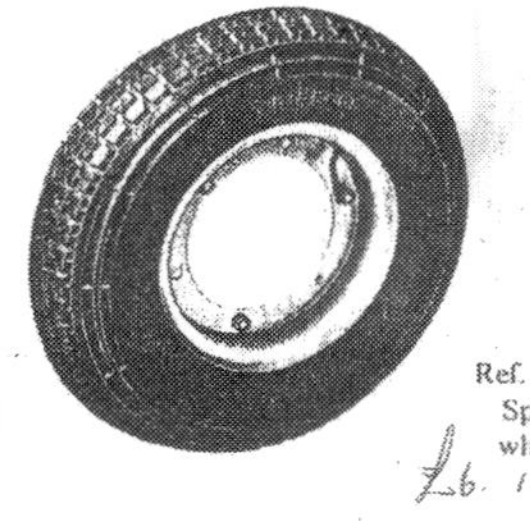

Ref. A45
Spare
wheel
£6 16ᵈ

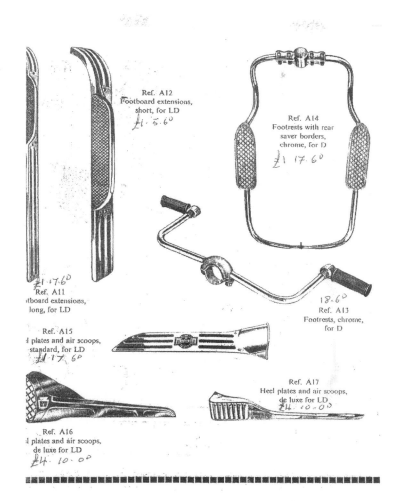

Ref. A12
Footboard extensions,
short, for LD
£1 5 6

Ref. A14
Footrests with rear
saver borders,
chrome, for D
£1 17 6

Ref. A11
tboard extensions,
long, for LD
£1 17 6

18 6
Ref. A13
Footrests, chrome,
for D

Ref. A15
d plates and air scoops,
standard, for LD
£1 17 6

Ref. A17
Heel plates and air scoops,
de luxe for LD
£4 10 0

Ref. A16
d plates and air scoops,
de luxe for LD
£4 10 0

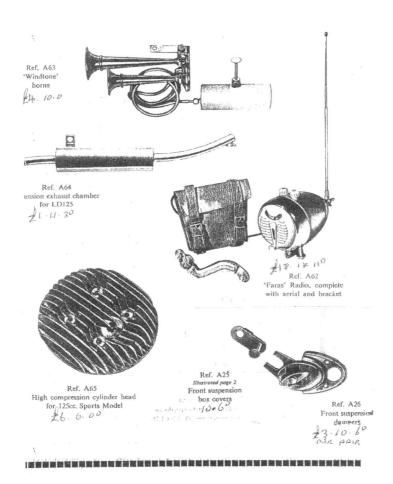

Ref. A63
'Windtone'
horns
£4. 10. 0

Ref. A64
ension exhaust chamber
for LD125
£1 - 11 - 3ᴰ

Ref. A62
'Faras' Radio, complete
with aerial and bracket
£18 · 17 · 11ᴰ

Ref. A65
High compression cylinder head
for 125cc. Sports Model
£6. 6. 0ᴰ

Ref. A25
Illustrated page 2
Front suspension
box covers

Ref. A26
Front suspension
dampers
£3 · 10 · 6ᴰ
PAIR PAIR

54

Here is another example of accessories available for your scooter. They were also made in green tartan and plain colours. Complete machine covers were also available with or without windscreen pockets.

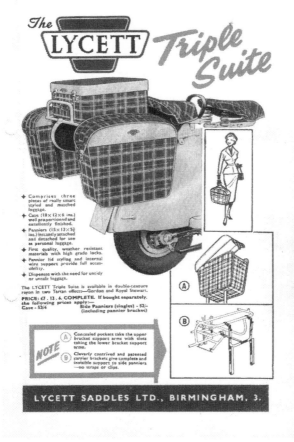

Brooks England Limited, West Midlands — after writing many times to your company, I assume you have no objections to me doing so. If you have any problems, please contact me.

I would not be exaggerating if I said there were hundreds more accessories available to fit the Lambretta scooters, other than those shown in the Lambretta Accessories catalogue. A couple of useful items for winter time were handlebar heaters that ran off the battery on the scooter. Handlebar muffs and a cover over your legs that fitted to the leg shields was also available.

If a screen was fitted to your scooter you could have a radio that was fixed to the handlebars with a bracket. On the early models Mark I & II, you could have a rear carrier with a spare petrol tank Ref: A110 or a luggage compartment Ref: A126. The early Vespa 125 models had a spare petrol tank that fitted in the spare wheel that was attached to the rear carrier. One Vespa I worked on had a spare petrol tank clipped over the centre footboard tunnel. Petrol stations were springing up everywhere, so in the end you did not need a spare tank to travel in and around the UK. Two accessories that are most sort-after today are the clock that fits in the glove box and the radio on the handlebar on the LD, and LDB machines.

The chrome accessories made in England were much better than the Italian made ones, because the Italian ones soon went rusty if you did not keep them clean with a good coat of wax polish.

Lambretta scooters were sold worldwide, in fact to 183 countries. Even at the rate of production — one every fifty seconds — they could not keep up with demand. Some countries produced the scooters themselves, with the help of Innocenti who arranged to clear the ground, build the factories, supply all the machines to make the scooters and give technical back-up to get the show on the road. With the vast amount of scooters made, of course, there were bound to be some troubles and many modifications. Quite a lot of trouble was caused by lack of servicing and some dealers were not doing the work right. A common problem was the torsion bar seizing up, which would mean taking the engine out, i.e. a great deal of heat was needed to free it, just because someone had not greased it. Likewise, the stand pin would seize, just for the lack of a drop of oil.

The front tyre would wear to an upside down V shape (this V shape turned up the other way) because the tyre was under recommended tyre pressure. Plugs fouled up a lot because of the amount of oil used, 1/2 pint to the gallon until Filtrate made proper two stroke oil. The best plug I found was Lodge HH14; it could stand the heat and not back fire.

There were many modifications to the kick start on Mark I & II. The aluminium pedal on the Mark 1 suffered if left loose on the clamp bolt, the splines would shear off. A steel one replaced it with a Mark II type. This was not quite right so a third one was produced; all had different pedal rubbers. Bearings replaced bushes. The kick start quadrant was modified about three times, along with the gear it meshed with. Other parts modified were, a quadrant stop pin, which was fitted to stop damage to the kick start case which would then leak oil.

On the Mark II and Mark 2½, a crack appeared on the frame cover just by the choke control and petrol tap. It was caused by the little lug that was cut out to grip the panel beading rubbers. When this first happened new frames were fitted, but later on the frames were repaired by welding up the lug and crack. All the work was done free of charge by Lambretta Concessionaires Limited, at Wimbledon.

Who would have guessed such a little cut out would cause the frame cover to crack. The later LDB and all LI and TV had no cut outs to hold the panel rubbers. The cracks are shown in red on the photographs below.

The 1957/58 D's and the LDB were the best of this type produced. The B stood for battery model. The D also had batteries and they could not be called DB's, as Aston Martin had that prefix. The reason Innocenti put batteries on the UK Scooters was because it was a requirement by law to have a parking light switched on if you were parked on the road at night. The vehicle had to be parked in the direction of the flow of traffic, so people could see your red light as they approached your scooter/car. The street lights, way back then, were nowhere near as good as they are today.

The Mark III had the best silencers/crankshafts and they had double ball bearings fitted. The right-hand one was lubricated by the oil in the gearbox and the magneto side one with grease. The grease could be changed by pumping more grease in with a gun. The bolt at the top of the magneto flange had to be undone to let the old grease out, if you did not undo the bolt when pumping grease in, it would force its way past the oil seal into the area of the stator plate. It could then stop the spark to the plug. The barrels were very hard wearing and this type of cast iron was called black diamond. When a re-bore was required, the engineers doing the re-bores moaned because the barrels being so hard, would wear out their cutters quicker. The piston had a special coating which helped to prolong its life.

A dual seat was available for these models but they were not very popular as you sat up quite high on the scooter so you could reach the petrol tap and choke. The other one sat lower and had cut outs each side so you could reach the controls.

STANDARD model £124 : 17 : 11 plus £29 : 19 : 6 P.Tax P/SEAT EXTRA
Battery Lighting Model £128 : 18 : 7 plus £30 : 18 : 10 P.Tax P/SEAT EXTRA

Courtesy of Mrs Edna Calder - Director of Lambretta Concessionaires.

DEALER TECHNICAL SHEETS.

 [INNOCENTI]   INFORMAZIONE TECNICA No. M/8   12.1.56

Lambretta 150 cc.
Starting Group

It has been found that a slight variation to the kickstarter pedal, as illustrated in the enclosed sketch, makes starting easier. Therefore, beginning from the engine No.143001, this part has been modified.

The new catalogue numbers are as follows:

- Kick Starter pedal   12111046   becomes   12111091
- Rubber protection   12110437   becomes   12110438.

Pre-modifica   Post-modifica

Pre-modifica   Post-modifica

Courtesy of Mrs Edna Calder — Director Lambretta Concessionaires.

Most people only had a service between 3,000 and 5,000 miles due to the cost. Round about this mileage, the scooter required a decoke and a new small end bush fitted as they wore out quite quickly, because of the heat of the engine. The modified bush had two extra holes drilled in the bottom to let more oil in. These had to line up with the two holes in the con rod. This did prolong the life of the bush. The clutch pull rod also had a short life. If over a period of time, the customer continued to hold the clutch lever in at traffic lights or at a standstill. In the end, the rod would pull through the bearing and all the ball bearings could enter the gear box. Needless to say it did not do the gears any good, which meant a major engine strip down.

The diagram below shows the latest modification to the right-hand footboard and panel on the later Mark II because of the bigger kick start body and the even bigger kick start on the Mark III. Both panels were altered at the back to take chrome grills. These panels had slots in them; the early panels had holes for the plastic grills to fit into.

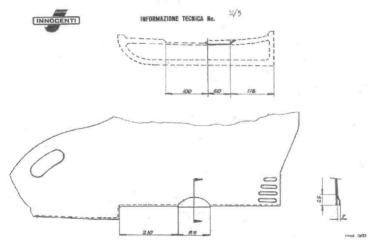

Courtesy of Mrs Edna Calder — Director of Lambretta Concessionaires.

The Mark I LD machines were fitted with aluminium handlebars and should have had a plastic sleeve fitted, where it was clamped to the aluminium bracket on top of the forks.

The Mark II had steel chromed handlebars along with the Mark 2½, but there may have been some Mark II machines with aluminium handlebars. All the Mark III machines had steel painted handlebars in white paint. Any of these handlebars could be fitted to your scooter.

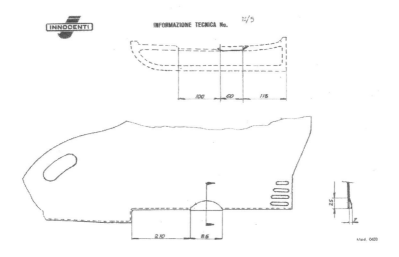

Reference Technical Sheets below S/3 & S/20

 INFORMAZIONE TECNICA No. S/3 13.7.56

Lambretta 125 and 150 cc.
Handlebar tube

The handle-bar tube of the above model, made of "peralluman"
light alloy, has now been replaced with a steel tube.

Therefore:

- Handlebar tube No.11770222 becomes part No. 11770230

This modification starts from:

Engine No. 150.850 (150/LD model)
  "   "   46.200 (150/D ")
  "   "   259.770 (125/LD ")

. and does not affect interchangeability.

 INFORMAZIONE TECNICA No. S/20 13.12.58

"Lambretta" 125-150/D and LD
Tube handlebar

Be informed that we are now in the
position to supply the handlebar tube 11770230 in both types, chromed
and painted.

The painted type, which is for the machine of 1957 production, with handlebar cowl, must be ordered as spare by quoting the
same code number followed by the letter A (11770230/A).

Courtesy of Mrs Edna Calder — Director Lambretta Concessionaires.

CHAPTER 3
A CHANGE IN MY LIFE

Jan on her brand new LI 150 Series I Lambretta outside her home on the Wells Estate, Epsom, Surrey.

Lynn on her TV 175 Series I Lambretta taken on holiday at Hopton-on-Sea, Norfolk with Jan.

A club run to West Wittering, Sussex. What a relief to get off that saddle. Lying in the sun, "Where is my lunch dear?"

A club run to Canterbury, Kent. Peter and Shelia with their LDB 150. Chris Mitchell with his LI 150 and Peter Clarke on Dick's TVI with screen and wiper. I was taking the photograph.

Our club on the beach at East Wittering, Sussex Not as good a beach as West Wittering, Sussex.

Our Club's favourite watering hole on way to and from Littlehampton, Sussex.

Club holiday in North Devon, with a visit to Lynton and Lynmouth.

Club outing to London Zoo, with Dot and Tom Howard, Harry, Lynn Beadle and her sister Sue, Ken Gotham, Jan and Dick. We are not sure of the girl's name on the end.

CAMPING AT ILFRACOMBE

Our camp site at Ilfracombe, North Devon. We had a great holiday and the weather for most of the time was fine. Almost ready for our long trip back home.

INTRODUCING THE NEW LAMBRETTA TV 175 SERIES I

Courtesy of Mrs Edna Calder — Director Lambretta Concessionaires.

THE WORLD'S FINEST SCOOTER

Lambretta
TV 175

The Sportsman's super Scooter

Anywhere and Everywhere . . . on every occasion . . . Comfortable and Fast.

Suspension:	Suspension by means of variable pitch helical springs coupled to hydraulic shock absorbers. Front and Rear.
Bodywork:	Elegantly styled handlebars, totally enclosed controls and illuminated speedometer.
Engine:	Engine Unit swinging on Silentbloc of ample range. Engine cooling by forced air through centrifugal fan.
Gear Box:	Four speed gearbox with patented roller type engagement.
Brakes:	Expansion type brakes with finned drums: Front hand controlled, Rear pedal controlled.
Frame:	Large section high resistance tubular frame.
Carburettor:	Carburettor with special air intake chamber. Diaphragm controlled flow to carburettor giving improved engine output.
Exhaust:	Specially designed exhaust silencer ensuring a high silencing effect and low power absorption.
Ignition:	Flywheel magneto ignition with external H.T. coil.
General:	Interchangeable 3.5 x 10 in. wheels. Headlamp incorporating main beam, dip and parking light. Direct current horn, constant note. Rear Brake stop lights.

SPECIFICATION.
Single cylinder 2-stroke engine, centrally mounted.
Stroke: 60mm.   Bore: 60mm.   "Square".
Capacity: 170cc. — 4 speed gearbox.
Output: 9 H.P.
Maximum speed: 65 m.p.h.
Tank Capacity: 1⅜ gals. (inc. 1½ pt. reserve).
Fuel Consumption: 94 m.p.g.
Unladen weight: 242 lbs.

LAMBRETTA CONCESSIONAIRES LTD., BEVERLEY WORKS, KINGSTON-BY-PASS. S.W.20

Courtesy of Mrs Edna Calder — Director of Lambretta
Concessionaires.

When I first saw this advert for the new TV 175 Series I, I just had to buy one as soon as possible. It looked fantastic with totally enclosed handlebar controls, dual seat as standard, bigger wheels and brakes, front fork dampers, plus being a larger scooter, this gave more room when riding two up. The weight diference from the LDB 150 was an extra 48lb (21 kilograms) and only 22cc more in capacity. The power output of 6hp for the LDB 150 up to 9hp for the TV I, made the all round performance so much better; coupled with better lights and stop lights, as standard and a most elegant handlebar layout.

Much has been said about the TV 175 Series I, probably by people who have not owned or ridden this model. For my part, I had one from new for four years and so did two other people in our scooter club; not once did these machines break down. The torque damper was designed to slip under very hard throttle action, or a hard down change, to protect the clutch and chain. Apart from servicing the only other work carried out was to decoke the engine from time to time.

Early models were all cream and had adjusters on the handlebars and slots cut in the side panels to let more air flow to the engine. The later models were coffee/cream, no slots in the panels and no adjusters on the handlebars. This model also had a much better rectifier and wiring loom. The very last models had the same tank and petrol tap as the TV 175 Series II. The dual seat on the TV I was quite narrow and hard and could be exchanged for a TV II dual seat, free of charge, if required. Yet again, Lambretta Concessionaires Limited thinking about their customers.

This model had orange stop lights along with the Vespa GS 150 and Fiat 500 cars, but had to be discontinued because orange flashing indicators were being fitted to cars and stop lights had to be red for all rear lamps.

On the early TV 175 Series I Lambretta, the magneto side ball bearing was changed to a roller type which gave much better service.

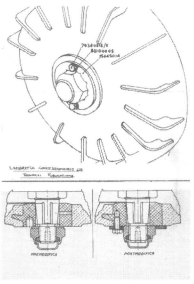

The silencer would get clogged up quickly due to the ratio of half a pint of oil to a gallon of petrol. This problem could be eased by drilling into the back of the silencer near the tail pipe with a large drill, right through all the baffles inside, then welding up the hole on the outside. The hub nut could come loose if

Courtesy of Mrs Edna Calder — Director Lambretta Concessionaires.

not done up tight, 127lbs (57 kilograms) on a torque wrench. It was advisable to get a lock plate kit fitted if it was an early model. This would have to be done at a Lambretta Dealers.

The early TV 175 Series I did not have a splash plate fitted to the stand, later on some had a shallow type fitted. A full size plate was soon brought out which made it a little difficult to fix the bridge piece screws and nuts.

I attached a small magnet to the socket screw driver which held the nut and washer in place, better than grease. I would say this was the most used tool in the Lambretta kit, as it was used to undo all carburettor clamp bolts, leg shields, footboard nuts and petrol tank strap bolts.

On the TV 175 Series I it was always best to turn the petrol tap off when you stopped the scooter to avoid flooding the engine. There was a hole from the float chamber up to the slide body, which was not necessary and a small aluminium plug was inserted. This was to stop the scooter stalling under heavy braking, also some TV 175 Series I's ran too rich and the main jet of 108 was changed to a 105. The Marelli spark plugs fouled up quickly, so Lodge 2 HLN was best to run on, later Champion N4 plugs were used.

The later TV 175 Series I had a grease nipple fitted to the Speedo drive for better lubrication.

A lot of vibration on the handlebars was due to too much free play. To overcome this, O rings were inserted on the tube before fitting the gear control. Another modification was to the horn bracket to make it more flexible to stop vibration damage. The front and rear brake shoes on later models had a spring plate fitted, to stop brake rattle, like on all LI shoes.

The early models had two screws holding the steering lock. If the lock had to be replaced, after the early stock of locks had run out, you would have to drill a hole in the centre of the handlebars and tap a thread into the hole, i.e. LI type lock and screw.

The internal mudguard on the front forks was not fitted on the very early TV or LI Series I, but were fitted to later models. When the forks were modified, a later internal mudguard had to be fitted. This had a part number: 19060160 in the improvements and variation catalogue. Customers could purchase this and fit to any scooter.

The TV 175 Series I and LI Series I had a shallower bottom fork cone with a spacer washer underneath it. When the stocks of forks ran out they were replaced with LI and TV II forks. The fork links would be replaced with nylon bushes, once stocks ran out. These changes were made for improvement and of course cutting down production costs. The changes made on all models were listed on technical data sheets with engine or frame numbers when the changes were made.

The fork stem was made with a taper towards the bottom so they would bend at this point to help save damaging the frame on a small impact. The bottom frame cone was made longer for the same reason not as I have read in some magazines; it was because the short cone came loose in the frame. I think I am right in saying the pattern forks had a straight stem and not made so well!

It was about this time that the Epsom Whirlwinds Scooter Club became involved in organizing their own road trials and going to other club events. The club went on a weekend camping trip to Lulworth Cove, I believe it was organised by The Kensington Scooter Club, and we met up with other scooter clubs and friends. We also went to a grass track meeting near Dorking, Surrey. It was at one of these events we first saw Go Karts racing. It was good fun and once again we had a great day.

BLOA British Lambretta Owners Association was up and running from March 1955 and every new scooter sold would have details about BLOA and a form to fill in if you wanted to join.

There were two types of this mudguard; the fixing bracket was made longer on the later ones to go with the later forks.

Early type Part No. 15060160 Two types LI I and TV I Later type Part No. 19060160 The two holes in the little internal mudguard are there so the bolts can be undone with a socket screw driver that is holding the front mudguard to the horn casting.

The steering lock on the left is a Series II type. The lock on the right is for Series I TV 175 only.

This picture is from a brochure, to advertise the new TV 175 Series I at the time. Some people thought it was me in my overalls out in Italy — I should be so lucky!

The real me on my brand new TV 175 Series I coffee/cream. The Eversure spotlight I fitted was wired into the battery circuit with a separate switch to help when riding on dark roads and was a godsend in the dark foggy nights.

I took my scooter to Lambretta Concessionaires in Wimbledon to have it sprayed red/black with a gold outline, it looked great. In April 1960, Jan and I became engaged, and I would soon be off to do my National Service. My niece is sitting on my scooter with my sister hiding behind her.

Courtesy of Mrs Edna Calder

HIGH FLYING FRENCH LAMABRETTA 125cc MARK IV
This scooter was made in France and brought over to England by Lambretta Concessionaires Limited because of yet

another strike at the Innocenti factory. People bought them because it was a Lambretta, albeit an older model compared to the LI 125 below. The one thing going for it, in my opinion, was the performance. It was as quick as the LDB 150. The engine was much the same as the LDB Mark III, but with a different carburettor and exhaust system. The saddles were similar to the NSU models. The bodywork was also different to the Mark III, along with all the handlebar controls and switches. There was no battery fitted and the centre stand and fittings were different. There were many other small differences on the scooter. The only colour I saw was grey/blue.

Courtesy of Jason Dean

LI 150 SERIES I

Some LI Series I were fitted with Marelli magnetos and HT coil B101E if you had a poor spark from the coil. The only other HT coil that would work with this magneto was a Bosch TJ6A6 or TJ6/6. These HT coils were also fitted to the LDB. The colours of these scooters were all grey or grey blue.

The first LI 150 Series I Lambretta I sold was a red and white frame breather type. My first road test on one was breathtaking to say the least compared to the 150 LDB, better in every way. These machines sold like hotcakes. There were a few things that were not too good. The magneto bearing was lubricated by the oil in the petrol, same as the TV 175 Series I, a step backwards from the LDB, but still had a reasonable life span if you used good two stroke oil — Filtrate being the best on the market.

The later LI had the air intake under the front saddle with a paper filter; these caused some problems with ladies on the back if they were wearing a skirt. The skirt could get sucked in the air intake and stop the scooter. Another problem was gloves and rag stored under the front seat.

I had a callout to a man whose scooter had broken down. Unfortunately, it took me a while to find him, (not a happy man). He had managed to get the scooter going, but it stopped after a few minutes. He did this about three times and was about a mile and a half further down the road. Still not a very happy man; in fact, he was downright rude. The engine had flooded so I pushed the scooter off the stand to give it a bump start, when I felt the rag under the seat and took it out. The scooter still would not start. I took the plug out (very black and wet) kicked the scooter over a few times, with the throttle wide open, put in a spare plug the man had in his toolbox and it started third kick. I left it running to make sure it was okay, while I put my tools back in the van and he just rode off without paying or saying thank you. I had no chance of catching him in the rush hour traffic, so I gave up and went back to work. Lesson learned. I was a lot more wary after that.

I received a phone call to pick up a crashed scooter from Epsom Downs, Surrey. To my utter dismay, when I got there it was my girlfriend's scooter, well smashed up. I took the pickup back to work and went straight to the hospital but was not allowed to see Jan. She was black and blue, no bones broken, but had a hairline fracture of the skull. I cannot begin to tell you how I felt at the time. Luckily, my mum worked in the hospital, and she could pop in to see how Jan was getting on and kept me informed. Thank goodness, as her father would not let me see her!

I was very pleased to have the scooter repaired and back on the road again for Jan so we could get our lives back to normal.

LI 150 Series I engine parts that deferred from Series II were magneto flange, magneto bearing, oil seal, crankshaft, barrel and piston, plus the cylinder studs, head cowl, front exhaust tube with silencer and tail pipe. The rear hub had a shallower cone, smaller battery and tray but they had the edge on performance over the LI Series II, but not quite so well on the MPG. You could not have it both ways. Other changes were bigger rear lamp, the vents in the rear frame covered in, the head lamp moved up to the handlebars and a new horn casting.

One of the best bolt-on goodies for the Series LI I/LI II and TV II was a sports silencer made by Carbury Garages Limited and was approved by Lambretta Concessionaires Ltd. It retailed at £5 5s 0d. It was a square type box with twin chrome tail pipe that came out of the box side by side and then the outside pipe twisted under the inside one just before the tail pipes fixing bracket. Later on, they made one for the Series III. This time it was a round type box, the performance was not as good as the standard box, unlike on the LI I, LI II and TV II where it did make an improvement to performance.

Pattern parts and accessories were big business, people like Mobyke Accessories, 93/99 Villers Road, London NW2.

Nannucci Limited, 2 Queens Road, Peckham, London SE15. Ken Cobbing, Waltham Cross Industrial Estate, Herts. Trauberman, 54 Crewys Road, London NW2. There were other smaller people who would go to Italy to buy spares and accessories to also sell to the trade.

Some of the pattern spares were OK, but most were not, like brake shoes, hubs, silencers, U pipes, clutch plates, gaskets sets, pistons, kick start shafts and pedals plus front forks. If a dealer sent in a pair of pattern forks for part exchange they would not be accepted, and the dealer would probably have to buy a new pair from Lambretta Concessionaires for the customer.

LAMBRETTA LI 150 SERIES I

Jan's LI 150 Series I Lambretta.

The LI 150 Lambretta scooters came in three colours for the UK market: off-white and either red, blue or turquoise.

This model had single saddles, like the LDB with more

power, bigger wheels, brakes and better lights. They were a joy to ride. Exide batteries were fitted as standard for the UK market, not the black type seen in some pictures, with totally enclosed handlebars like the TV 175 Series I. This gave them a very streamline appearance.

Lambretta Series I 125/150

The LI 125 Series I scooter came out a little while after the LI 150 Series I model and were about £20 0s 0d cheaper. They came in two colours grey or grey/blue, with single saddles. My customers wanted the LI 150 scooter and I never sold a LI 125.

My girlfriend Jan, at that time, had a new LI 150 in red/off-white and she had it re-sprayed in Ford colours yellow/black. Her first scooter was a blue Vespa 125. She liked the LI 150 a lot, apart from it being a little bigger compared to her blue Vespa.

Rakes Rodeo, Loughton, Essex 1959. This photograph was taken at the Cricketers Pub before our club rode off to Loughton, Essex, all dressed up as cowboys and Indians for the Rodeo weekend. Young Jimmy Goatham had an accident on the way to Loughton, Essex. A school boy ran out in front of his scooter and the club ended up in the private school while details were sorted out. The Fancy Dress Competition was a good result for our Club first and third places. Indians won cowboys took third place.

Grass Track Meeting near Dorking, Surrey.

As a club, we used to go to grass track meetings and this is where we first saw these funny little things on four wheels called Go Karts doing a demo race to see what people thought of them.

A few weeks after the Go Kart racing, Mike Smallbone and I thought we would have a go at kart racing and set about building our own model. Not long after we got started, Mike got his call-up papers so I had to go it alone. Five months later,

I received mine. By the time we had completed our National Service, our Go Kart was obsolete so that was the end to our move into karting.

This Go Kart meeting we attended was in Oxford. Once again, the weather was wet and cold and we were glad to get back home.

This was my last trip with the club to Newhaven, Sussex with Jan, Dot, Tom, Mike and Maggs, Lynn and Julian, before I started my National Service.
Mike had completed five months of his National Service by this time, but came out on this Sunday run with me as it would be my last trip for two years. Off to serve my queen and country.

COMPARISON OF LAMBRETTA SCOOTER PRICES.

In 1956 the Mark II LDB 150 cost approximately £160 0s 0d.
The Pillion Seat cost about £6.0s.0d. extra.
In 1958, the TV 175 Series I cost £209 17s 6d.
In 1959, the TV175 Series I cost £199 17s 6d.
In 1960, the TV175 Series II cost £189 17s 6d.

On top of all these prices, you had to find money for number plates, road tax, insurance, tax disc holder, L plates, petrol and oil, and maybe hire purchase payments, which was a big amount out of your wages, as wages were quite low in those days.

LAMBRETTA CONCESSIONAIRES LIMITED
BEVERLY WORKS, KINGSTON-BYPASS SURREY

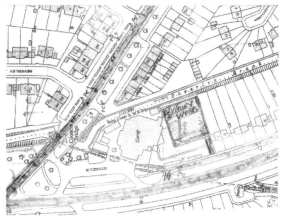

Courtesy of Ordnance survey

Lambretta's home, for a short while, was at Beverley Works, marked in blue on Beverley Way, new Kingston-bypass marked in red. Combe Lane, from Kingston, marked in green.

The site was too close to the row of, about 20 houses, as shown in photo below. The noise was also a problem along with getting in and out of the premises because of the bypass.

Courtesy of Peter Pooley

1960 LAMBRETTA SERIES II

Advertising leaflet for dealers.

Courtesy of Mrs. Edna Calder — Director Lambretta Concessionaires.

The LI 150/125 Series II had the same colours as the Series I. The main changes, as mentioned, were to the engine, carburettor, silencer and of course the headlamp moved up onto the handlebars. In the main, the scooters gave little trouble. In most cases, it was down to the person who owned the scooter and how they looked after it as to what troubles they had.

I had little to do with the Series II as I was in the army based at Aden and Hong Kong, serving my queen and country for two years.

Courtesy of Mrs Edna Calder — Director Lambretta Concessionaires.

A few of the TV175 Series II's were fitted with a brass flywheel with extra balance weights inside the flywheel. The tick over was so slow you could hardly hear the engine running.

1960 Sales brochure and price tickets for showroom display.

The LI 150 Series II only cost £5 0s 0d, more than my LDB 150 Mark 2½ in 1957.

The TV 175 Series II was also sold in two extra colours, ice blue with a tan dual seat and a very light yellow called straw. The blue colour was by far more popular.

This scooter was £10 0s 0d, cheaper than my TV 175 Series I in 1959.

CHAPTER 4
MY QUEEN AND COUNTRY NEEDS ME
MY TWO YEARS NATIONAL SERVICE
JUNE 1960

Here I am at the start of my two years National Service, when we were
first let home on leave. We had to wear our uniforms at all times. I
called in to see some of my teachers at Lynton's Lane Secondary
School, Epsom, Surrey.

DUNKIRK PLATOON
DEPOT HOME COUNTIES BRIGADE

Lambert Weston.
Folkestone.

Our Dunkirk Platoon group photograph with our brand new Sergeant Moody. I can still hear his words today as he came into our barrack room. "My name is Sergeant Moody, moody by name, moody by nature. You are my first platoon and you are going to be the best." As luck would have it, we were just! So we would see our mummy's again!
Courtesy of the Surrey Infantry Museum Surrey.

During our basic training at Canterbury, we were allowed home early on a forty-eight hour pass after six weeks, not ten as told when we first joined up. The reason given: we were doing very well in our training. I think it was more to do with the sergeants wanting their weekend's off.

As soon as I got home, out came my scooter and a quick dash to see Jan. Only to my utter dismay to find she was just about to go on holiday with her friend Mavis, on her Lambretta. There was no way I would stop her going as it would not be fair to Mavis. It was sad for both of us at the time. The only good thing was that I was allowed to ride my scooter back to barracks, as from now on we would be allowed home each weekend. I took an old friend from my school days back to camp with me, which helped with the cost of petrol.

When we transferred to Colchester, Essex, I was also allowed to use my scooter, which was great because I could get back to barracks in just over two and a half hours. If I had to go by train, I would have spent most of my time travelling. In fact, some of the boys did not go home because of that.

We left Colchester, Essex for Aden in January 1961. Travelling by train, through Surbiton, Surrey on the way to Southampton, which left me with a lump in my throat as it was where I had been working.

It was a few months later that Peter Clarke, who started the scooter club with me, immigrated to Australia and sadly we have now lost touch with each other.

NATIONAL SERVICE, JOURNEY BY SHIP TO ADEN

We sailed from Southampton on the 3rd or 4th January in the Dunera. The Dunera later became a school ship. On our way to Aden we stopped at Gibraltar, Malta and Cyprus after a very rough crossing of the Bay of Biscay. It was good to see the sun after we left Gibraltar.

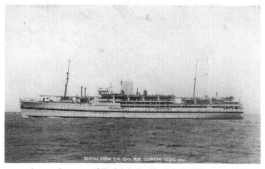

Postcard sent home of British India M.S. "Dunera" 12,615 tons —Courtesy of Surrey Infantry Museum, Surrey.

The journey took us down the Suez Canal to Aden. The weather was hot and the sea calm. The photograph is of Crater Town, our Barracks was about 4 miles away from here.

Aden — Panorama of Crater from Tunks — Courtesy of Surrey History Centre.

We were told brand new barracks had been built for us when we got to Aden. I cannot put into print what was said, when we saw what we had to live in. It would be a good six months before we would move to the new barracks.

My bed was opposite the door so I looked out onto the site of our toilets, which was just a long trench in the ground. We all sat in a line on a bench with a hole in it (very modern). Bed bugs were the biggest problem though.

My truck and me. The trucks had wire cages to protect us from any stones that were thrown when driving. I also had the job of taking the officers wives and families shopping, plus picking up food from the stores for the barracks.

Here we are on exercise in the desert. As you can see, very rocky and the track I drove along was not much better. I pitied the men in the back of my truck.

Now this is what you call a sandbank, with my truck under cover next to it. It was very hot in the day time and very cold and damp at night. The bushes and grasses only survive because it is so damp at night.

In the desert you not only have rocks and sand to contend with, but in some places there are salt flats. One minute you are OK, the next you have sunk up to your axles. I am pleased to say nobody was hurt when this happened. No it was not me driving, thank goodness.

At last, we have moved into our new barracks with air conditioning, flush toilets and showers. Just my luck, I was about to be sent up to the mountain camp.

Here we are at the bottom of the escarpment. The track we have to drive up is in the middle left of the photograph, and top left you can just see the track as we get near the top of the escarpment.

We move on to Mukera's which is our camp at about 6,000 feet and will be my home for the next three months. It is very cold at night. Most of our food and fuel is bought up by plane.

YEMIN BORDER

Almost at the top of the escarpment. Top left corner of photograph shows the most dangerous part of the track. It was made of loose rubble to raise the level of the track and was often damaged by the rain. Middle of the photograph shows three Land Rovers travelling up the track.

The top of the escarpment shows the clouds coming up from the valley below. Our camp site was about one hour's hard drive from the top over very rough tracks in between farmer's fields.

Our home in Mukera's for the next few months. The daytime temperatures were comfortable, but very cold at night.

On duty unloading stores from the Beverley cargo plane.

I was always greeted with, "You damage my aircraft, and you will be with us for a good few years before you get home."

MUKTERAS AIR STRIP

The Beverley Cargo Plane taking off in a dust cloud heading back to Aden. A cargo plane DC3 Dakota waiting its turn to take off next.

Our three months in the mountains were completed and luck was on our side for a change. We were flown back to Aden in less than an hour instead of two very long hard days driving by road.

We were only in Aden for a few days before leaving for Hong Kong on the S.S. Oxfordshire.

S.S. OXFORDSHIRE

Courtesy of the Surrey Infantry Museum.

Helicopter displaying our regimental flag.

As we were leaving the port of Aden for Hong Kong on the SS Oxfordshire, the RAF did a fly pass with our regiment colours which was a great tribute to our regiment for the way we had carried out our duties in Aden.

The S.S. Oxfordshire called into Colombo and then Singapore where a Ghurkha Regiment were waiting to be picked up for the journey to Hong Kong. I was assigned to them for the trip to Hong Kong and stayed at their barrack for a few days until I was moved on to Stanley barracks; my home for next few months.

My new home for three months.

I was in the third block far right middle floor. These barracks were the best I had stayed in.

As soon as we arrived in Hong Kong, we were told we had to buy civilian clothes and shoes to have a photo taken for our passports for our civilian flight home. Before that, three of us had two weeks leave due to us. Most of our time was spent in the NAFFI Club downtown and buying things to take home. We had a trip out on a ferry to the Island of Macua, which was very interesting. The flight home took about twenty-seven hours as we had to land twice in India, for some passengers to depart and others to join us for the flight to the UK.

Repulse Bay — best beach in Hong Kong.

The Queen's Royal Surrey Regiment in Kowloon on parade for the Queen's birthday. I am in the front row second left from the officer on the right.

Photograph taken by a friend.

We had only two weeks to serve when there was trouble on the border with China. The rice crop had failed and all the people were coming over the border for food. We would feed them and send them back, only for them to turn up the next day for more food. I bought as many sweets as I could for the children, which in hindsight was not my best idea. I did not have enough for all the children and felt bad when I saw the look in their eyes. The trouble was soon over and we were sent back to barracks and at last back to the UK.

CHAPTER 5
BACK IN CIVVIE STREET
LAST FEW DAYS IN ARMY AND DEMOB

At last, my two years in the army were completed and finally I was on my way home from Hong Kong to Stanstead Airport, Essex and then back to Epsom, Surrey.

Home at last; unfortunately, no Jan to meet me. It was Mick and Margaret's wedding day, and she was one of the bridesmaids. I was hoping to attend the wedding but, unfortunately, we were about twelve hours later than first expected. Plus, a very big hold up at Stanstead Airport Customs while they went through every item of kit we had brought back with us and having to pay duty on some items. The air was quite blue.

Jan managed to slip away early and, at last, we met up outside my house.

During the time I was in the army, my sister and brother had married along with many of our friends. Jan and I married the following year June 8th 1963.

Our club was still going strong, thanks to Jan and many others. They had been meeting regularly at the Cricketers Pub and going out on Sunday rides. The club had attended a Rally held by Chichester Scooter Club. Tom Howard and his driver had an accident, so his wife Dot had to ride their scooter home. The club also went camping for the weekend at Lulworth Cove, Dorset. It was suggested by the club that I take the reins again and I was very happy to do so.

My first job the following day, after getting back, was to get my TV 175 Series I going as I had to report back to Canterbury on Monday morning for final demob.

Jan sorted out my insurance and road tax for me, plus a gallon of petrol, so all I had to do was clean the plug and carburettor and fill up with petrol. It started after three kicks. A quick dust off and pump the tyres up and I was ready for the road. What a great feeling to be back home with Jan and riding my scooter once again.

On Tuesday, I went to G & R Garage Limited, Surbiton, Surrey to see everybody and started work the following Monday. To my utter dismay, the scooter side had closed down. The man left to run it while I was away had just walked out and left. My boss had retired to Malta, so I had to start back working on the cars which was a disappointment.

I had been back three months when George Savage from Kingston Scooters came to see me with an offer of a job. All be it a Vespa Dealer, but some other scooter servicing as well. I took up his offer, and had been working there for about five months when I bought a new TV 175 Series III before Jan and I got married in June. Our friends Dot and Tom who had been in the scooter club a long time also purchased a new scooter.

The TV 175 Series III Lambretta scooters were show replicas, in coffee and white. The registration numbers were 9077PJ and 9078PJ. They had a disc brake on the front, the first mass production of a two wheeler to have them.

So that was two new Lambretta scooters from a Vespa dealer this must be a first. Our two traded in Lambretta scooters were sold within two weeks. George was a very happy man; even so he would not stock Lambretta Scooters, which was very sad really because I liked working there so much. To George Vespa scooters were far better than Lambretta scooters. Even so we had lots of problems to sort out, such as the main bearings on the Sportique 150 model, clutches and cush drives also gave trouble.

Two things I liked about George was that servicing had to be done 100% along with repairs and the use of filtrate oils only on Vespa scooters in his shop.

It was time for me to start looking for a new job, but first Jan and I were getting married. Having nowhere to live after trying numerous flats, our dear friends Dot and Tom asked their landlord (Tom's sister) if we could share the house with them which was just around the corner from my work. The rent was reasonable, which we shared with Dot and Tom. Tom was best man at our wedding. While we were on our honeymoon, they decorated our lounge and bedroom for us, which was a lovely surprise. We were there quite a few months and had the garden looking good.

Jan was finding it very hard travelling to Reigate, Surrey from Kingston, Surrey on her scooter, so she told her boss she was going to leave. He was so shocked at the news that he found us a maisonette to buy in Morden, Surrey much closer to Jan's work. He also was co-owner to Christies Estate Agents, in Cheam, Surrey!

We moved into our new maisonette in November 1963, in Tudor Drive, Morden, Surrey, our first step on the ladder to owning our own property.

One of my first jobs in our new home was to clear the back garden of three-foot-high grass, and also pull down an old shed, ready for my new Banbury garage — a safe place to keep our scooters.

About the same time Jan and I moved into our Maisonette, I went to work for Lambretta Concessionaires Limited in Croydon, Surrey. This is where I met Vern Laville; he was the foreman in the service department. I first met him on my Lambretta training course at Wimbledon back in 1956 and we remained friends until he sadly passed away quite suddenly in 2008. Apart from  being a great shock to me, it also meant we would be unable to compile our combined experiences at Lambretta Concessionaires Limited together. Vern being there much longer than myself would have had a lot more tales to tell, along with Brian Gibbs. When Brian got together with Mike Karslake, all hell was let loose. All in good fun of course.

The last time I was with Brian, outside of work, was at the Surbiton Scooter Rally held at Chertsey, Surrey. I entered in the Concourse D'Elegance, as it was called then, as I had not long re-sprayed my scooter. In those days, to make it fair, an entrant had to enter at least two other events before the Concourse event. So, a quick dash around on the grass and then a good clean up, and too my surprise I won first prize.

It was about this time I called into G & R Garage Limited, to fill up with petrol and catch up with old friends. I was told that the boss had retired and left the garage to all the workers until the lease ran out, which was about three or four years. I would have been included as well if I had not left. At that moment in time I was upset, but looking back now I took the right path and have no regrets.

I had been working at Lambretta Concessionaires Limited, Croydon, Surrey for some time when I called back again to see how things were going at G & R Garage Limited. The news was not good, one person had already left as they were not making any money and the lease was almost up; the building was due to be demolished. I was glad I was not there when it happened, as I have so many good memories of the place.

A NOSTALGIC VIEW OF TROJAN LAMBRETTA WORKS

Aerial photograph of the TROJAN WORKS, Purley Way, Croydon, Surrey before Lambretta Concessionaires Limited took over. Courtesy of Aerofilms

All ten photographs of Trojan works were kindly given to me by the late Mrs Edna Calder — Director of Lambretta Concessionaires for use in this book.

THE MAIN ENTRANCE INTO TROJAN WORKS.

The Lambretta sign is above the office block.

Showing buildings to the left of the main gate, most of these would be taken down now.

THE NEW WAREHOUSE WITH LAMBRETTA TRANSPORT READY TO DESPATCH NEW SCOOTERS TO THE DEALER NETWORK

Showing transport and Trojan bubbly cars ready for dispatch to dealer network.

LI Series II waiting to be cleaned and checked for any damage before going out to the dealers.

Large batch of LI 150 scooters and some TV 175 Series II's ready for dispatch.

The electric hoist in the new warehouse, capable of carrying 6 scooters
at a time up to the floors above.

A vast stock of LI 150 Series II's on the middle floor of the warehouse.

The top floor of the dispatch warehouse showing LI 150 Series II and in the foreground the 150 rallymasters fitted with tv 175 dual seats.

Lambretta Concessionaires produced these commercial outfits for the RAC in their blue colour and with special battery lighting for their radios. They also produced one or two for Nivea hand cream company. Courtesy of Mrs Edna Calder — Director of Lambretta Concessionaries.

CHAPTER 6
THE FINAL HOME OF LAMBRETTA CONCESSIONAIRES LIMITED, CROYDON, SURREY
SERVICE DEPARTMENT

THE NEWLY-BUILT and ultra-modern Service Spares and Accessories division.

Newly built Lambretta House

The day would start by clocking in and finish by clocking out and doing the same at lunch time. We also had to record the time spent on each scooter we worked on. When completed Brian Gibbs would road test the machine and if passed the scooter was clocked off the job ready to do the same on the next one.

It took quite a time to get spare parts from the main stores, so it was decided to have a service store by the workshop to speed things up. There was a stack of bins with all nuts, bolts, washers, screws and more outside the service office. The mechanics just took what they needed and wrote on the job sheet the word sundries small, medium or large. It was then charged accordingly.

The Service Department was at the front of Lambretta House on the left-hand side, as you looked at the building, along with the reception which was still looked after by Brian Gibbs. I first met Brian at Wimbledon. His job was to book all work in.

Lambretta House first looked like the photograph with all the scooters waiting for repair inside the big door. It was very cold in the winter because of all the glass and high roof.

Working in a glass house was not good for mechanics trying to work on cold wet scooters. This brand new building was not watertight, some of the glass panels had to be replaced. In the meantime, all we had to keep the weather out was plastic sheeting, which did not stop the snow blowing in one November night in 1964. On arrival at work we were greeted with at least one inch of snow covering the whole workshop. We set about clearing and mopping up the snow as quickly as possible. Two space heaters were hired to help dry out the service bay. The following day, we were greeted with a very cold and damp workshop. All our worktops, tools and ramps were covered in rust and it took all morning to clear up the rust, before we could start working on the scooters again.

TEMPORARY SERVICE DEPARTMENT

The Strike — 1965

We were moved to this new building as a major rebuild was carried out to Lambretta House. This brand new building was glass-sided to let in as much light as possible, which made it quite hot in the summer. One good point was that it was fitted out with a modern hot air duct system, so we should have been nice and warm in the winter. If only that was true; if they kept their word, the heater would have been working before the winter set in and the strike would not have happened. After several nights of heavy frost, the workshop became very cold. We were all fed up with working in the cold. I arrived late on my scooter that morning as the roads were extremely slippery from the overnight frost. I was greeted with "Don't take your coat off because we are not working in these cold conditions, we are going on strike." After about two hours and much debate, we all went home.

When we all returned the next day, we heard Mr Bennett had recommended the sack for all of us, but instead space heaters were installed until the ducted heater was working thank goodness, and we all returned to work.

HARRY YOUNG, Service Manager, Lambretta Concessionaires. ERIC ALLVEY, Stores Manager. ARTHUR LINGHORN, Assistant Stores Manager.

Mr. Bennett was the service manager for many years. He left the firm quite suddenly and Harry Young took over. Mr. Maurice Knight was the sales manager, Eric Allvey store manager, and Arthur Linghorn the assistant store manager

The photo shows a line of scooters in the temporary Service Department which backs onto the main stores. The department would be here for some time until the new front of Lambretta House was completed. McLaren cars had moved into their part of the building.

My best memories of Brian Gibbs, before he sadly passed away, was one morning as Vern arrived in his Vauxhall car covered in dirt. Brian and a few other people were looking in the boot of the car and absolutely rolling about with laughter. All they could see when looking in the boot was their feet, as the base of the boot had rotted away and dropped onto the road on the way to work.

The story unfolded that as Vern was driving to work, a car behind him flashed his lights so Vern put his foot down a bit more. The car was still flashing him so he pulled up at the side of the road. The man behind him got out and said something dropped out the back of your car about three miles back. That was when he discovered he had lost all his tools, spare wheel and other items. A new base for the boot was made and welded that day ready for Vern to go home that night. I can still picture today Brian rolling on the floor with laughter.

The front of Lambretta House has changed again, no petrol pumps this time. The Service Reception would be at the front to the left of the big doors, on the right-hand side of the building. The big doors on the left-hand side were for access to the rear of the building. The Lambretta Service Department ran down that side, with the service area for ISO cars and general workshop alongside Lambretta Service. McLaren cars were at the rear of the building.

The Final Home of Lambretta Concessionaires

A very small part of the vast stores area, you can just make out the two bins at the front full up with LDB silencer and tail pipes. The photo shows part of the trade counter. I spent many an hour or so there in the past, before we had our own stores in the Service Department and stock control office.

LAMBRETTA ACCESSORIES AND SPARES trade
counter deal with some of the hundreds of customers
seen every day.

**STOCK CONTROL SECTION at Croydon which
deals with more than 2,000 orders a week.**

All the spares for the early models up to 1959 were taking up too much space at Croydon, Surrey. Trident of Bristol was appointed as main distributors for all these spares. Horner & Sons of Manchester had a large stock of early parts including TV 175 Series I Lambretta parts, so it freed up more space for current model parts.

The Service Department was large with about 12-14 ramps for

scooters. Each mechanic had their own bench and tool board, as shown on the front page of the Official Lambretta Manual.

Lambretta Staff

Other people I came in contact with while working in the Service Department were Nick Hands — sales representative, John Shepherd — welding department, and Ken Peters — technical representative. Eric Pollard and Mark Cooper both worked in the service department and have sadly passed away. Mark Cooper lived around the corner from where I lived in Epsom, Surrey.

Other people I worked with were Chas DeLacy, Nick Barnes and John Lee who came from the Isle of Mann. John ended up working for Homelite chain saws service department alongside the Lambretta service department.

Ken Hurlingshaw worked in the Service Reception after Brian Gibbs. He was often in the service area looking at what we mechanics were working on.

With the help of Rex White and others Ken complied The Lambretta Manual of Performance Tuning and Conversions.

Many dealers would call into the service department if they had a problem with a scooter or wanted a flywheel re-magnetised on the quick or just for a chat. This is how I met Roy Cary of Roy's of Hornchurch and landed up working for him in Hornchurch, Essex.

One other person I must mention is Mick Hayman who worked for Lambretta Concessionaires Limited, after I left and worked for Suzuki as a technical representative until he retired. Mick still owns a SX 200 and has helped me out with some vital parts on a couple of occasions; to which I was most grateful.

GT 200 LAMBRETTA SCOOTER.

This scooter could possibly be one of Lambretta Concessionaires
Limited Demo scooters, but not with that dual seat which is off a TV
175 II and the centre part of the panel was sprayed in violet.

It was the fastest standard 200cc scooter on the road at the
time.

Fewer than 15,000 GT scooters were built before the SX
200 came into production. Both models were all white in
colour from Innocenti and colours to panels were sprayed at
Lambretta Concessionaires Limited, Croydon, Surrey. Some
dealers did their own colours and design. The SX 200
Lambretta was a good scooter to ride and better looking than
the GT, but not as fast. The GT 200 was the fastest standard
scooter at that time.

MAJOR CHANGES AT LAMBRETTA CLUB GREAT BRITAIN

The sudden departure of Bob Wilkinson was a huge shock to everybody working in the service department.

LCGB had to find a replacement general secretary. I believe the task fell to Pete Davis who was working for Lambretta Concessionaires Limited at that time in 1969.

Good old Rex White ran the club for a while in 1970, but was unable to commit himself to more time as he was involved with the late Barry Sheen and the Suzuki Racing Team. John Ronald and his brother Norman, plus members of the Nottingham Scooter Club took up the challenge for about three years. I believe two other clubs helped out at one stage. Much later, Kev Walsh, plus a very good committee, took over the task.

I would like to take this opportunity to say a very big thank you to everybody that has run the LCGB and Jet Set Magazine.

Thanks to Norrie Kerr for all his hard work on the production of Scooter & Scooterist Magazine and for his excellent parts business which is still operating to date.

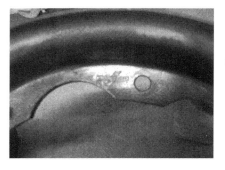

Photo of Innocenti wheel rims fitted on all Lambrettas for the UK market. There was a great amount of pattern rims on the market; some of them were okay, some were not a good fit to the hubs.

A dealer could obtain these sheets free of charge, from Lambretta Concessionaires Limited to cut the cost of adverts in their local papers. There were pages for all models. All the dealer had to do was pick out the one he wanted to go with his advert.

LAMBRETTA FREE STOCK BLOCKS SHEET No. 14

Below is the leg shield sticker for the early LI 150. Please note the tyre pressures are not right for the UK market, they should read 18 — 28 and 34.

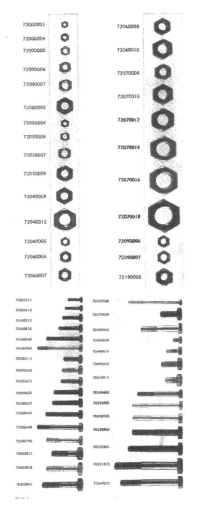

All Lambretta spares had a parts number, but were all in different books for each model. For quick reference items like nuts, bolts, washers, circlips and oil seals were put on sheets shown on the left.

On column one top left, the first two digits, i.e. 72 explains the item is a nut and the last two 03 gives the size of the nut 3mm in size.

When ordering spare parts the dealer had to write down what he wanted i.e. silencer and the part number 19518510.

If the wrong number was written down the dealer would receive the part that the number related to. The part number meant the same in any language.

Each model had its own part number LI Series I and II started with 15 and Series III started with 19.

The displays of bolts started with 70 and the last two numbers give the length of the bolt.

All carburettor parts started with 0041. All magneto parts

started with 0084.

The only true way of knowing what part was fitted on each model was to refer to the parts book and modification sheets supplied by Lambretta Concessionaires Limited.

Whenever a new model came on to the market, the dealer would be sent brochures of the models, plus accessory lists, prices and spares lists.

After the early Series III, all Lambretta control cables were now being made without oilers on them, to cut costs on the production models. There were a vast stock of oiler type cables to be used up, at the Lambretta Concessionaires stores and all dealers stocks, before the new cables went on sale.

Have you experienced all the thrills and advantages of owning a **Lambretta**

In the first place, it gives you an independence such as you have never known before, enabling you to travel to and from work unhampered by such snags as queues and time-tables, allowing you to explore the countryside and far-distant places in your spare time. Secondly, the LAMBRETTA provides you with by far the most economical means of getting around on the roads today, costing you considerably less than a penny a mile to run. With a new 150 'SLIMSTYLE' LAMBRETTA you can really be somebody. This beautiful, aerodynamically designed scooter will be the envy of all those less fortunate than yourself. And it is backed by a second-to-none after sales service network throughout the UK and Europe – a service that has been praised over and over again by 2,500,000 satisfied owners of LAMBRETTA, the world's best selling scooter.

Get your hands on a new SLIMSTYLE **Lambretta** now!

The best scooter for all round performance.

The TV 175 Series III was the best scooter by far; it had great all round performance. The lights were better, less vibration than the Series II as it had larger engine mounts. **The first TV 175 Series III had smaller disc pads fitted, but were soon changed to the size of pads we use today.** This meant the disc brake was remade to take the bigger pads. The front brake cable was changed from the heavy duty type to the standard Series III type.

A fibreglass front mudguard was fitted, but this gave rise to an unusual problem. People who lifted their scooters by the front mudguard when moving the scooter, on the centre stand, hence got a hand full of front mudguard. As stocks ran out, they would be replaced by metal ones. If a mechanic in the service department did this, they were in a lot of trouble.

It has been stated by some people that the GT 200 engine mounts collapsed, but this was not correct. The right hand one did sag quite a bit and the rubber compound was changed to help in this problem.

It was also stated that Lambretta Concessionaires Limited

128

fitted a double engine mount to stop this problem. In fact, this was done for competition work; racing. At the same time, there were quite a few dealers making double engine mounts for their competition scooters to improve the handling at speed on the racetracks. The first double engine mounts made at the Concessionaires were made to fit into a sleeve (no welding). Later on, the two mounts were welded together; this kept the cost down. Racing also brought about the reversed pull cable for the disc brake.

GT 200 SILENCER PROBLEMS

A great deal has been spoken about the GT 200 silencer some true; some not. Going back to 1963 for the start of the TV 175 Series III, with a much longer silencer than on the TV 175 Series II. Both silencers had the same type of main bracket, which did show signs of fatigue on some of the TV 175 Series III. I believe the GT 200 also had the same main bracket on their silencer to start with although, it was different internally. The later silencers for both models had a stronger main bracket. Much has been spoken about vibration being the only cause of the main bracket failure. There are three points I would like to make.

FIRSTLY if the silencer was grounded this would cause stress to the U pipe, silencer and tailpipe fixings; which should be checked and all the nuts should be tightened up as soon as possible to avoid further problems.

SECONDLY the silencer was quite long with only one main fixing point. When an extra fixing point was added the silencer was much more secure, but only when it was bolted up tight.

THIRDLY a large amount of pattern silencers were sold at the time. The metal was thinner and not made to the same standard as the Innocenti silencer. When a pattern silencer was sent to Lambretta Concessionaires for repair or exchange it would be rejected under the terms of guarantee. The dealer who sent it would have to sort out the problem with the customer. Badly grounded silencers were also rejected under the terms of guarantee.

The first modified silencer from Innocenti came with a bracket to fit under the crankcase. It was fitted to the silencer by two holes drilled in the flat moulded part of the silencer body and fixed with two 6mm bolts and captive nuts. A hole was drilled and tapped in the small aluminium square of the crankcase, marked in red on the photograph. The silencer bracket was secured to that point by a 6mm bolt. All the later crankcases had a large moulding to take an 8mm bolt for the modified fixing bracket that is now welded to the silencer.

GT 200 SILENCERS

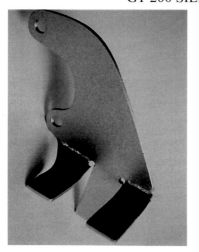

Early type main bracket fitted to Series II and Series III silencers. The red line on the photograph shows were the cracks started to appear.

MODIFIED SILENCER BRACKETS

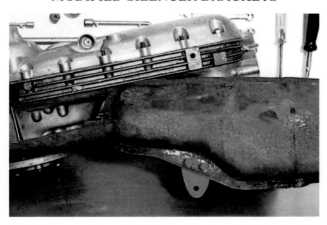

Early silencer with modified bolt on bracket which fitted to the crankcase marked in red.

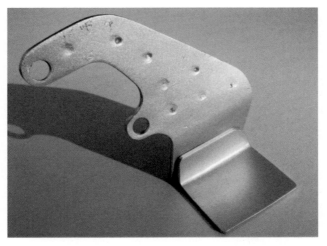

This modified main bracket was made by Trojan Engineering for all early silencers with failed brackets under guarantee terms. These brackets plus any damage to the tailpipe fixing were also repaired. Both parts of the bracket were welded together, and then attached by welding to the silencer body.

Courtesy of Peter Pooley. Early modified bracket for bolting to silencer and crankcase.

Early pattern silencer with extra bracket hole too big and not in line with crankcase fixing 8 mm bolt.

Pattern Silencer with later fixing bracket — same as SX and GP silencers.

SILENCER CLEANING

In the early days of LD Lambretta scooters, a blow torch was used to burn out the carbon from the silencers.

On LI Series I and II silencers, as stated earlier in the book, a large drill bit was used to drill through the baffles to ease the gas flow then weld up the hole on the outside of the silencer. In some cases, caustic soda was used to try and clean out silencers. I myself would not advise this, better to buy a new silencer. On all Series III, silencers a steel cable attached to a drill was all that was needed to clean out the carbon from the tail pipe.

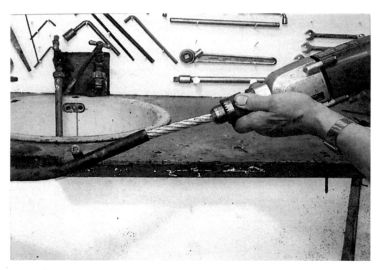

Push the cable into the tail pipe before starting up the drill, on a slow setting and stop the drill before pulling out the cable.

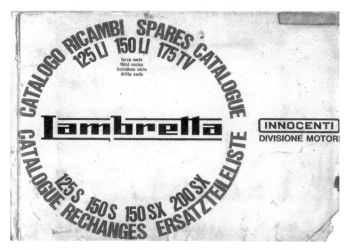

The cover of my parts book, just like me getting on a bit now.

Part No.	Refer to	Description	Model
00412209		Main Jet 108	GT
00412352		Carburettor SH1/20	GT/SX
00412353		Pilot Jet 48	GT/SX
00412407		Main Jet 103	SX
00611097		Speedometer C- (5.0.1.	SX
19518010		Exhaust tube	SX
19550150		Motif 'Special'	SX
19610060	19710030	Silentbloc	GT/SX
19610160		Crankcase	GT/SX
19611003		Cylinder head gasket	GT
19611004		Induction manifold	GT/SX
19611012		Long stud for induction manifold	GT/SX
19611017		Gasket for induction manifold	GT/SX
19611030	19611060	Cylinder and piston assembly	GT
19611040	19611050	Cylinder and piston assembly	SX
19612018		Gudgeon pin	SX
19612310	19612350	Piston assembly 66.0	GT/SX
19612320	19612360	Piston assembly 66.2	GT/SX
19612330	19612370	Piston assembly 66.4	GT/SX
19612340	19612380	Piston assembly 66.6	GT/SX
19616022		Springs for carburettor hose	SX
19618060	19918060	Silencer	GT
19620015		Clutch spring	GT/SX
19630001		Gear group	GT
19630003		1st gear	GT
19630004		2nd gear	GT
19630005		3rd gear	GT
19630006		4th gear	GT
19630029		Kickstart pedal	SX
19650170		Motif 'Lambretta'	SX
19650190		Motif 'X 200'	SX
19650200		Motif 'Tv 200'	GT
19655072	19955093	Rear flash 'Tv 200'	GT
19655076		Panel flash L.H.	SX
19655077		Panel flash R.H.	SX
19655150		Dual seat RED	SX
19655180		Side panel L.H.	SX
19655190		Side panel R.H.	SX
19918070		Bracket for silencer	SX
42010005		Cylinder base gasket	GT/SX
42011002		Cylinder head	GT
42011002	42911002	Cylinder head	SX
42011003	42911003	Cylinder head gasket	SX
42012018	19612018	Gudgeon pin	GT
42012024		Piston ring 66.0	GT/SX
42012025		Piston ring 66.2	GT/SX
42012026		Piston ring 66.4	GT/SX
42012027		Piston ring 66.6	GT/SX
42012140	19612150	Crankshaft	GT
42912150	19612150	Crankshaft	SX

The relevant list for the GT 200 parts marked with*. The other parts
are for the SX 200. The first GT 200 pistons, part number was
42012090 std 66mm and went up to 42012120 for the third oversize.
See list for early TV 175 engine mounts part number 19610060. All
later engine mounts had a different part number 19710030. The cost of
a complete and painted disc brake back in the 1960 was £18.0s.0d.

1964 — The Year of the Pacemaker.

We have now moved on from the standard Lambretta 125/150 LI Series III and quite a few years of the special Lambretta scooters. This model started as a white special, then onto the metallic grey Pacemakers at a price of £177 10s 0d and £179 17s 6d, with red or blue panels.

The dealers mark-up was £34 12s 9d. Out of this the dealer had to do a pre delivery check, fit the number plates and road test the model. They also had to carry out the first 500 mile service free of charge. The Pacemaker with blue panels was by far the most popular scooter.

Much has been spoken about the Pacemaker gears; in fact I do not think anybody has an original set now, as the third gear teeth broke along with damage to the gear group. They were all changed to the 125 special gear boxes. I have heard it said, that the third gear was thinner, that is why it broke. This was not true as you would have had to have a mighty thick shim to make up the difference from the standard gear shim.

The other fact that was reported was the gear was smaller, but how would that fit to the gear group? In fact, the third gear had smaller teeth to make a different ratio, but lack of strength was the trouble, because of that they would break off under a hard down change from fourth gear.

Apart from that, the Pacemaker gave very little trouble and was a very good scooter to ride. Over 100,000 of these models were made.

The scooters mentioned are what I call the true specials with the same headlamp and later type panels as the TV 175 III and TV 200 scooters. These were followed by LI 125/150 specials, some with LI front mudguards, some had round headlamps and some were continental models without batteries, which were not normal UK specification.

1964 — Lambretta Concessionaires Limited stock of the Pacemaker.

The two people in the picture are Nick Barns on the right and (I believe) Alan Kimber's brother on the left. I was taking the photograph just before we were told, in no uncertain terms, to get out. I was unable to take any more photographs after that, which was a shame as all we wanted to do was look at the fantastic view of all the new scooters. What a sight with all floors full up. I am glad I did not have to clean and polish that lot before they went out.

The photographs are of the warehouses where all the scooters were kept until distributed to the dealers. I believe there were four floors in each building. Most dealers did not like red panels, as you can see from the pictures. The name Pacemaker possibly came about because of the group, Jerry and the Pacemakers. The group came to Lambretta Concessionaires Limited, Croydon, Surrey to learn how to ride the scooters, possibly for publicity. I was away the week they came to Lambretta Concessionaires; such a shame!

SERVICE DEPARTMENT

Because people sat on their scooters and drove them off the stand it would pull the bolts in the frame and the stand would hang down and rattle about.

In the service department, we fitted the LDB stand spring which was a little bit shorter than the standard spring and brought the stand back up to where it should be. In bad cases, the frame had to be repaired and welded where the bolts had started to pull through the frame strut. On refitting, we used a large thick washer behind the bolt to help spread the load. Another part we used was a stud from the Mark II LDB kick-start unit. This was a little longer than the standard LI crankcase studs, used for the tail-pipe bracket on all the LI/TV scooters to allow for fitting a nyloc nut. Another trick used was to heat up the tail pipe when bolted up fully on the engine and let it cool down slowly. This was done to take out any tension in the pipe, so as not to put strain on the tail pipe stud.

Engine frame tube modification was carried out in the Lambretta Service Department, Croydon.

While on the subject of welding, on some of the TV 200 frames the engine mount tube came away from the frame. This was due to bad welding at the Innocenti factory. The frames were welded and a lug was made up and welded to the frame, with a hole in the middle for the HT cable to pass through.

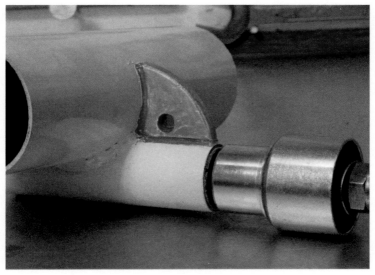

The photograph shows where the lug was welded to the frame and is indicated by the red line, plus the welding to the engine mount tube to the frame.

If you were fitting a sidecar to your Lambretta scooter you had to have this gusset welded to the frame for added support, along with alteration to the leg shield struts to make room for the sidecar bracket. The right way to fit the sidecar and frame bracket is shown in later pages. The Spanish Lambretta scooters had a similar support bracket.

There is a special engine mount tool to remove, and refit both types of engine mounts. Also, there are two types of frame cones, one for the standard LI 125/150 type mounts, and the other for all engines with larger type mounts. If you had a standard LI 125/150 and you wanted to fit the larger mounts you must also fit the 200 type frame cones. Failure to do this may cause damage to the crank case and put stress on the engine mounts.

1964 A very smart looking little scooter.

SPECIFICATION

Capacity	98 cc	Tank capacity	
Bore	51 mm	(inc. reserve)	6.2 litres (1 ¼ galls)
Stroke	48 mm	Max length	1690 mm (66 ½ in.)
Compression ratio	7.5 : 1	Max width	630 mm (25 in.)
Max output	4.7 h.p.	Max height	1030 mm (40 ⅓ in.)
at crankshaft		Wheel base	1190 mm (47 in.)
Max speed	76 km/h. (47 mph)	Height at saddle	770 mm (30 ¼ in).
Consumption	1.87 lt/100 km (150 mpg)	Number of seats	1 + 1

ENGINE Single cylinder two stroke, forced air cooled, petroil lubricated.

GEARBOX 3 speed on rear wheel drive shaft. Hand controlled. Gear ratios: 1st 1 to 4.8 : 2nd 1 to 2.867 : 3rd 1 to 1.857.

IGNITION Flywheel magneto ignition with external H.T. coil.

TRANSMISSION By chain drive enclosed in crankcase and running in oil bath, transmission ratio: 1 to 3.214 (45/14 Z).

SUSPENSION Front: by means of trailing links with helical springs inside fork legs. Rear: swinging engine unit with helical springs and hydraulic shock absorber in parallel.

WHEELS Interchangeable. Rims in pressed steel. Tyres 300 x 10.

BRAKES Front: by expanding brake shoes with hand cable control. Brake drum diameter 150 mm (5.92 in.) Width of lining 22 mm (0.865 in.) Rear: expanded brake shoes, pedal controlled. Brake drum diameter 150 mm (5.92 in.) Width of lining 22 mm (0.865 in.).

ELECTRICAL EQUIPMENT Feed through 6v flywheel magneto. Headlamp with dual filament bulb 6v 25/25W and Festoon 6v 5W. Rear lamp fitted with red gem reflector and dual filament lamp 6v 3W for parking and " No Plate " illumination. 15W for Stoplight. Speedometer illuminated by Headlamp Festoon bulb. Light switch with engine cut-out button. Horn 6v AC.

FRAME Steel built for strenght - yet remarkably light.

WEIGHT In running order, 80 kg (176 lbs).

CENTO

It was a bit of a surprise to us in the service department in 1964 when a new model that had been talked about turned up in the workshop.

It was a very light scooter with a frame similar to that of the Vespa. It turned out not to be quite as robust. Cracks started to appear from the panel, retaining lug round towards the petrol tap and from the other side towards the choke control.

At first, it was put down to the frame being too stiff. So one section was taken out, plus the strut under the plastic toolbox inside the frame. A further modification was made to the side panel retaining lugs, they were made much longer and the inside edge was welded. This did the trick as there was no more trouble after that. The rear hub bearing was a sealed unit type and soon failed, the modified bearing was similar to the LI type.

The lay shaft also failed as it was a little too short for the first gear to run on. This also had to be replaced.

Some of the crankshaft twisted on the crank pin, so they were modified along with the magneto side bearing, which was a small roller type. This was changed to a large ball bearing type, which was housed in a new magneto flange and a more robust steering lock was fitted to later models. Also, an extra bracket was fitted to the silencer on the magneto housing side.

The last thing I can remember going wrong was that the magneto started to produce too much power to the lights, which was soon overcome with a new coil that produced less power. I also made a 12 volt conversion kit for these models. The 12 volt battery was housed in the toolbox. The cost was probably too high for these lower priced scooters, so it did not sell well.

I must just add, not all Cento's were affected by all these problems and to date I have seen two Cento's with the old type frames and no cracks.

Cento £115 17s 6d J125 £129 10s 0 0d Starstream £152 0s 0d

On the very latest Starstreams, the rear part of the frame was a different shape. The same body as the latest little 50cc scooters. The rear lamp body was also a different shape and would only fit properly to these scooters. The rear lamp part number was 20063008 and I believe the gasket for the rear lamp body to frame would have been 20163011. The bulb holder and rear glass was the same as Cento J125 and Starstream.

The Cento was made as a cheap form of transport, but to my mind too many corners were cut to keep the cost down. Apart from that, it was a good little scooter once all the modifications were carried out.

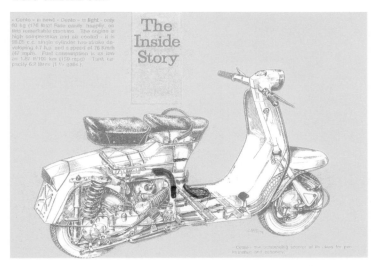

The small panel retaining bracket for locating the panel is clearly shown in red, which was not long enough; this is where the crack started from, blue marks where the bracket was extended to.

The frame strut in the toolbox marked in green was removed along with the centre panel on the frame tunnel. This was done to make the frame less ridged. Also marked in green are the extra stand support struts. These were put in to help strengthen the frame, because people were sitting on the scooter with the stand down and rode the scooter off the stand, which caused damage to the frame stand support strut. Vespa models also suffered over the years with the same problem to the frame.

Another special project job was to convert a road going Cento to travel on water on two large floats. The engine had to be made water tight and a paddle wheel made and attached to the rear hub, but it kicked up too much water and stopped the engine. The floats were too thin, which meant the whole thing sat too low in the water. So the floats were cut in half, more material added and re-fibre glassed around the sides, also the air intake for the fly wheel was improved. The paddlewheel was replaced with an impeller type unit to improve the performance and steering.

Fancy a trip on the Thames? Not me. Too low in the water for my liking; the floats were made a lot deeper after this trip.

125 Starstream and super J4 speed scooters.

The promotion photograph of a 125 Star stream and no the model
sitting on the scooter was not part of the sales package.

The J125 — Starstream and Super J4 speed did not suffer with
the same problems as the Cento; in fact, the super J4 speed was

a delight to ride, taking into account it being a small frame scooter.

Over 17,000 Cento's were produced. It is pronounced Chento. The combined 125 models produced were over 37,000 and the production of all these models ran from 1964 until 1969.

Lambretta Concessions looked at an outboard disc brake for these models. The one tested was not very good and the next step up in size would have been too expensive. So the idea was dropped.

Lambretta Service Department Croydon

I was involved with the service side at the motorcycle shows in London. When a customer had a question about the engine, I had to strip the engine down so they could see how it worked. I also had to show how to fit the front crash bars correctly and the right way to fit the rear one with a carrier and backrest. One question that was frequently asked was the good old miles per gallon. I had to keep saying time and time again the mpg was taken at 30 miles per hour. This prompted Lambretta Concessionaires Limited to run an Economy Competition at Brands Hatch, Kent and the next year at Mallory Park.

The service department were also involved at the Southend International Rallies in Essex to look after any scooter that had a problem, all free of charge; which was a real help to scooterists from abroad.

Lambretta Concessionaires Limited was involved with Go-Karts and racing them. From the late fifties onwards outboard motors for boats, chain saws, the production of the Trojan Bubble Cars, and ISO cars from Italy. McLaren Racing cars were manufactured at the back of our Service Department, which was great for me as the man that did the welding occasionally helped me out, if the boss was not around!

I was involved with making the 6 volt battery conversions for the RAC and police scooters with radios. The RAC also had box sidecars fitted with a complete spray job in their blue colour. The frame struts that supported the leg shields had to be cut off and welded back the other way around when fitting the side car bracket.

Lambretta Concessionaires Limited also made two special scooters for people with artificial legs, one of them had a rear brake fitted on the left hand side; both had the leg shields cut out and a section welded in so they could keep their leg straight.

I was also involved in making 12 volt lighting kits. To start with, all the old 6 volt stator plates that had been sent back to Lambretta Concessionaires Limited under guarantee were cleaned up; new lighting coils were fitted and rewired. Additionally, contacts and condensers, if required, were replaced — plus new stator looms.

All the old 6 volt rectifiers that were no good were stripped out, cleaned, holes drilled in them for air flow and a new Lucas rectifier fitted in the case. The diode was fitted on to an aluminium heat sink which was made from the aluminium extrusion used in the Trojan factory and not, as I have read in a Scooter Magazine, that it was a moped front hub. All the bulbs, wire, nuts and bolts were in the kits. All the dealer had to do was fit it as and when required.

There was a service exchange department for barrel and pistons, rear dampers, horns, speedo heads, silencers with modified brackets, forks and frames. If an exchange frame was needed, you were required to put the exchange frame number in the log book. On some of the 4 volt and 6 volt flywheels, the fan would come lose, so they were cleaned in a special type of acid to remove all the dirt then put into aluminium cleaner and came out looking like new. The fan was then refitted to the flywheel with four screws and re-magnetised before being sent back to the dealer.

LAMBRETTA TROJAN WORKS SCOOTER WAREHOUSE

Courtesy Mrs Edna Calder and Associated Iliffe Press.

The scooter warehouse shows LI 150 Series III and LI 150 Special Scooters. In the photograph there are a few scooters that have been repaired in the service department. In the front row, silver J 125 registration number: AUM73C and a GT 200 registration number: CVF11B. They will be delivered back to the dealers along with the new scooters.

CHAPTER 7
LAMBRETTA CLUB GREAT BRITAIN IN FULL SWING

Brands Hatch Lambretta Economy Run Sunday 6th December 1964.

After completing scrutineering, to make sure that your scooter was the right model and capacity for the class you were entered in, plus having your tank drained and refilled with a gallon of HI FI and the tank sealed, we were ready to start. We all had to lap the circuit at an average of 30 miles per hour. We were timed over the finish line each lap. If you were early or late, a point was deducted each time from your final petrol consumption result.

When the machine had to go onto reserve you were required to switch your lights on and a marshall would then follow you until you ran out of petrol a note was then made of your mileage. My first stop after going round the circuit for over four hours was to run for the toilet. The marshall that followed me was good old Chuck Swonnel.

I was pleased to learn later on that I had won the TV 175 class doing almost 134 miles to the gallon. I think what prompted Lambretta Concessionaires Limited to run this event was that so many people complained about their mileage per gallon. Sometimes it was hard work explaining you had to ride at 30 mph to achieve a good mph figure.

J. Miller GT 200 120.528 mpg
Innocenti claim 100 mpg
R. Sedgley TV 175 III 133.837 mpg
Innocenti claim 110 mpg
K. Raynsford LI 150 III 144.252
mpg Innocenti claim 124 mpg
R. Wilson Model F 125 153.363
mpg Innocenti claim 128 mpg
N. Ronald Cento 147.56 mpg
Innocenti claim 145 mpg

I believe there were about 50
competitors taking part in the
competition.

1964 A copy of the
certificate given to each
competitor on
completion of the
Economy Trial.

A big thank you to all the Marshalls
and scrutinizers, not forgetting Bob Wilkinson and the LCGB
staff that carried out the time-keeping.

LAMBRETTA WORKSHOP

I was involved in helping to produce the First Edition
Lambretta Home Workshop Manual, with the late Vern
Laville. A great deal of time went into producing the manual
in a way to help the scooterist, but at the same time not to take
work away from the dealer network.

The manual cover shows a customer's scooter I was working
on at the time. The disc brake needed adjusting and there was
no speedo cable, plus the rear of the tail pipe had been cut off
the standard box, which will not help the performance.

Over 100,000 copies were sold to Lambretta Owners and I was very lucky to be presented with one of the very first off the production line by Bob Wilkinson.

There were several editions of the manual printed over the years.

The Workshop Manual was produced by Kingsley Press.

Each mechanic had his own bench and vice. After work had finished, you cleaned your ramp and bench, plus all your tools and put them back on the board before going home.

This photograph was taken at the same time as the one used on the workshop manual. In the background, you can see two of the work benches and tools. There are no ramps as the photographer was trying to make it look like a home workshop.

The two photographs used in the Home Workshop Manual were by Cowdray & Moss Ltd for Lambretta Concessionaires Limited 1964 61181/2Courtesy of Mrs Edna Calder — Lambretta Concessionaires Ltd

The Bats Scooter Club Scrambling Event, Elstead, Surrey. —
1964

Our club used to attend these meetings, but did not take part at this
time.

All lined up ready to go, not all of them made it to the finish line.

Brands Hatch Sporting Trial — 1965

Back at Brands Hatch once again and by the look of Jan who is standing behind me, it was yet another cold day. This time it is for a Sporting Trial. I am not looking too happy, unlike a very young Christine Jackson on my right. It was a very muddy event and no surprise to me I did not do very well as I only had standard road tyres on the scooter. I had a good time and was glad I hadn't damaged the scooter.

It was a very cold run down to Brands Hatch from Epsom, Surrey, and no better on the run home, especially with muddy tyres.

Epsom Lambretta Club members outside Dave Gilbert's house in Ewell, Surrey. This photograph shows Dave and a very young John Wood, who is still a very valuable club member today.

These photographs show many members sitting on one scooter — no wonder the stands hung down on Lambretta Scooters.

LAMBRETTA CONCESSIONAIRES LIMITED, CROYDON, SURREY. TROJAN WORKS.

Trojan also produced the Bubble Car, but time was running out for this type of vehicle and the entire workforce on the production line were made redundant.

Sometime later, the factory received a very large order for the bubble car and everybody was contacted to return to work. Most of them did and production was started up again until the order was completed.

Lambretta Concessionaires Limited also had an engine exchange service for the Trojan 200, £40.0s.0d. Net to dealers.

SPECIAL PROJECT

I was involved in modifying a chassis of a Lambro Three Wheeler for a milk firm to see if it would be feasible for a milk float. This would require extending the chassis by about three feet. The chassis was cut forward of the spring stops and two extension pieces welded in. A longer prop shaft had to be made along with brake pipes, wiring loom, hand brake cable and the silencer was also extended. The last items to be completed were new front spring hangers that were welded to the chassis. All the welding was carried out in our service department by John Shepherd.

This was a major conversion to the basic model and in the end I believe the cost was too high for the milk firm looking at it. That was the end of that project. I often wondered what happened to this conversion. The Concessionaires had started to make an FLI 175 engine into a V twin 350cc engine, but once again the cost would have been too high, so it was dropped.

ITALIAN ISO CAR

The Italian made ISO Grifo and Rivolta cars were Bertone styled with 5½ litre V8 Chevrolet engines. At the time, they were the fastest production four door saloon in the world. It was rumoured that the Beatles had at least one of these cars.

McLaren Can-am Series cars had a lot of success on the racing track.

I am not sure what brought about McLaren Cars taking part of the Lambretta workshop space at Croydon, Surrey apart from it being a light modern building with good access to main roads. It meant Lambretta Concessionaires Limited had to move the service department at least twice, so they could bring all their equipment in. On Lambretta Concessionaires Limited's part it would help to cut the cost of running the building.

LAMBRETTA CLUB GREAT BRITAIN SOUTHEND INTERNATIONAL RALLY 1965

The LCGB club held a celebration dinner in the Garons Banqueting Suite for the bosses and staff from Lambretta Concessionaire's and their partners. All LCGB Club Secretary's and their partners were also invited. Free drinks were available for one hour before the dinner was served.

All other club members at the rally were then allowed in for the dinner and Fancy Dress Dance. The photograph shows Epsom Whirlwinds Scooter Club members with Vern Laville and Eric Pollard. After the dance was over, it was off to Southend Pier for a Bowling Competition. Vern, Eric and I were very drunk and really unable to take part.

Southend, Essex International Rally 1965.

Epsom Lambretta Club all lined up to display their new knitted tops
made by Jan and her Mum. Bottom picture shows everybody watching
the prize giving for all the events of the past two days. The weather
was very kind to us. Vern, myself and two others mechanics from the
service department were on duty, doing running repairs to any scooter
that needed attention.

Scooterists from all over Europe came to these events at
Southend to enjoy themselves. No big headlines in the papers

as there were no punch-ups.

There was going to be a rally in London; all clubs would have to help with the marshalling of the event. In the end, it was called off as the police were not happy about the threat of Mods and Rockers causing trouble.

LAMBRETTA AT BUCKINGHAM PALACE

H.R.H. The Duke of Edinburgh was presented with a Lambretta 150 Special scooter by Innocenti during the British week in Milan for use of his office staff.

I went up to Buckingham Palace to carry out the first service, making sure that the machine was running well and fitted the number plates. This was carried out at the front far right of the palace. The scooter was serviced regularly. When I left Lambretta Concessionaires to work for Roy's of Hornchurch, I believe Chelsea Scooters carried out the servicing.

Lambretta Owners Service Book to keep all records of service and repairs.

THE SERVICE BAY at Lambretta Headquarters, Croydon.

Courtesy of Mrs Edna Calder — Lambretta Concessionaires Ltd.

Tony, Terry and myself trying to look as if we were working on the scooters in a mock-up of the service department.

This may have been for a motorcycle magazine. We did not like this picture as it did not reflect the orderly way in which we normally worked.

The early TV 175 Series III engine mounts were sprayed white, not plated like they are today, which may have lead some people to believe they were made with white rubber. One has to ask why Innocenti would go to all that expense to produce white mounts when all other products in rubber were black or grey.

This photograph shows Chris & John Wood on his GT 200, and me, Jan and little two month old Stephanie in the sidecar. We were taking part in a Road Trial in October 1965.

I made special engine mounts to take the extra weight of the sidecar, it comprised of 1½ engine mounts both sides; I also used them when racing my scooter.

This was my first run out after a complete overhaul and re-spray after fitting the Bambini Sidecar. The colour was metallic blue and white.

Lambretta Club Great Britain held a New Year's Eve Dinner Dance at The Londoner Hotel, London in 1965. It was open to all Lambretta Scooter Club secretaries and their partners, plus staff from LCGB and the bosses of Lambretta Concessionaires Limited.

Everyone had a great time, and a chance to meet and get to know other scooter club members. The food was great and the drink flowing. Dancing was top notch also. Apologies for the wine stains on our invitations. Shows what a good evening it was.

PRODUCTS TAKEN ON BY LAMBRETTA CONCESSIONAIRES LIMITED

Homelite Chain Saws turned out to be a very good product and had the same sort of service set up as Lambretta Concessionaires Limited.

A log cabin was made as a mobile office for use when they attended agricultural shows around the country to demonstrate their saws and service back-up. It was also used at a Snetterton 12 hour Lambretta event and a van was also fitted out as a mobile workshop which would go to forest areas to carry out repairs and service work.

Most of the servicing and repairs were carried out at

Croydon, Surrey in the Lambretta Service Department, by John Lee from the Isle of Man. He had worked on Lambretta scooters before taking on the servicing and repairs for Homelite Chain Saws. The smoke and noise became a problem for us and the office staff upstairs. All the testing had to be carried out at the back of the building.

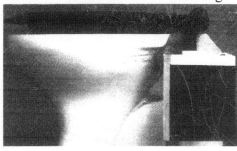

☒ Left PAN-AIR the revolutionary toilet air conditioning unit—the latest manufacturing undertaking of Trojan Engineering Ltd

☒ Centre A general view of Trojan's machine shop at Trojan Works, Croydon showing some of the 600 machines

☒ Bottom Two of the bank of ten Bullard Multi-au-Matic Vertical 6 or 8 spindle chucking automatics

Toilets, would you believe it, from the Trojan factory. It was a good idea, but not sure whether it went into production. Product of Trojan Engineering and Lambretta Concessionaires Limited.

Photographs — Kingsley Press for Lambretta Concessionaires Limited.

Product of Trojan Engineering and Lambretta Concessionaires Limited. The Trobike was produced as a lightweight fun-bike to go in the back of your car. It had an American Clinton engine much the same as fitted in the Go Karts that Lambretta Concessionaires Limited sold and raced in the Fifties.

SCOTTISH SIX DAY MOTORCYCLE TRIAL.

Three Lambretta scooters were entered and all three finished. The picture tells its own story. The Road Going Rally Master followed on from this fantastic success.

RALLY MASTER

One option was to fit a 400 x10 tyre to the rear hub if the gearing was a little on the low side for road use. Also available was a special gearbox which comprised of LI 125 first and second gears and LI 150 third and fourth gears with a specially manufactured gear group. I am not sure if it was made at the Trojan factory or by Innocenti.

LAMBRETTA ARE NOW part of the "British Way of Life", being used for example by police forces for patrol and traffic duties.

The picture shows one of many Lambretta scooters made to police specification with special 6 volt battery lighting and with a two stage charging rate for operating their radios. They also had some standard 150 machines, just for patrol work, and when they came in for their first service, some had done about 1,500 miles on the clock. The back tyres were bald. I did wonder just what sort of patrol work they were doing with the scooters.

This picture shows the dual control Lambretta scooters on the back of the truck. It must have made it more difficult for the person learning with all that extra weight on the back.

TROJAN FACTORY, CROYDON, SURREY.

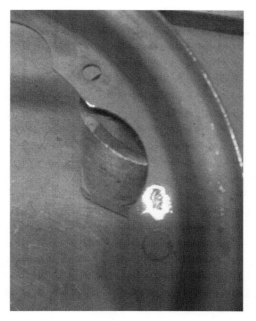

The Trojan factory also manufactured wheel rims for the Lambretta scooter. They had a little 'Trojan Helmeted Head' stamped on the rim to identify them from the pattern ones. Many dealers purchased them as a complete wheel, as the price was very good and then would split them up. That way they made more profit

The Lambretta Rally Van was always in attendance at all LCGB events.

The Lambretta Filtrate Sprinter. It was ridden by a young lady in white leathers, NO records were broken.

Only the men gained records.

The Lambretta Filtrate Sprinter using my modified disc brake. In the end, a drum brake was used to cut down the weight.

Filtrate was unable to claim any records because of the lady rider. They could have used, a then young Nick Barnes, who was a very good rider, so it must have been done for publicity.

The young lady holding this lightweight sprinter was Madeline Parker.

NEW FILTRATE SYMBOL IS A SIGN OF OUR TIMES

"Is it a bird? Is it a plane?" they used to ask in the old Batman films when the hero came swooping out of the sky to right a few wrongs. There have been a lot of similar questions posed about the new Filtrate symbol shown here. Whether you see it as representing a wave in the tide of our fortunes, a large drop of an unnamed lubricant, or a stylised "f" for Filtrate, the device is here to stay.

When a company has been in business as long as Filtrate, a change of image is always difficult, in fact it can be quite painful to say goodbye to the old familiar typefaces and letterheadings. The trouble is that graphic design moves with the times, and it's important to keep a bright, punchy appearance on notepaper, vehicles, tins, drums and promotional material.

The new symbol, or corporate logotype as the advertising boys have it, has been a year in the creation. During this time the company looked at and rejected a score or more visual identities which didn't fulfil the brief.

The final choice was felt to be distinctive and authoritative; memorable; capable of being applied to stationery, buildings, packaging, transport vehicles and apparel. To us it's also visually pleasing, and we hope you will be able to live with it too, because you're going to see a lot more of it in the future.

BRAKE SERVICE

When servicing scooters with disc brakes, the lever was given a good clean and grease applied to all moving parts. The slots in the back plate were cleaned with a fine file. The disc locating holes were drilled out with a 13/32 drill bit. The retaining spring was refitted along with new softer disc pads. This made the brake more efficient. I made a longer lever and rerouted the brake cable on my disc brake. To give me more stopping power, when racing my scooter.

Filtrate also made a special two stroke oil for outboard motors fitted to boats.

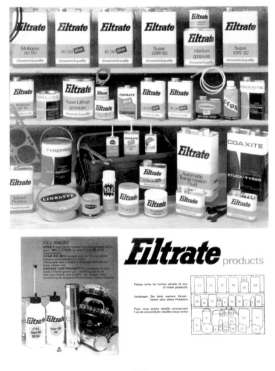

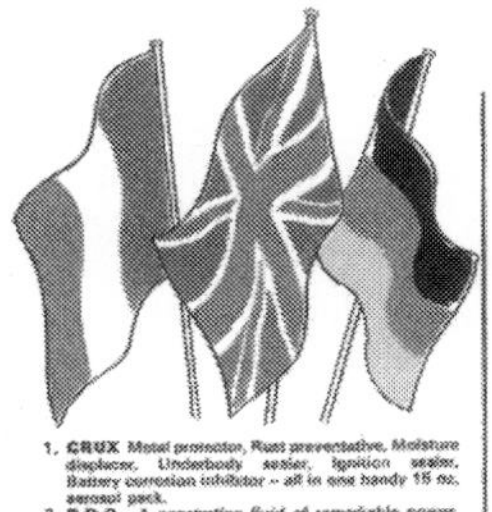

1. **CRUX** Metal protector, Rust preventative, Moisture displacer, Underbody sealer, Ignition sealer, Battery corrosion inhibitor – all in one handy 15 oz. aerosol pack.
2. **P.D.Q.** A penetrating fluid of remarkable power. Helps free rusted up parts – "Pretty Darned Quick", In 5 oz. Aerosol Pack.
3. **PLUS COMPOUND** Oil additive. Contains a concentrate of colloidal graphite – improves lubrication – eases running-in.
4. **POLYOIL** A very useful general purpose household and workshop oil.
5. **LINKLYFE** (in solid form) A unique chain lubricant, will not fling off, resists dirt and moisture. Solid Linklyfe must be heated so that the chain can be immersed in the molten Linklyfe, this ensures absolute penetration of the lubricant into the pins, rollers and plates.
6. **TYREPRIM** An anti-adhesive – prevents tyres becoming stuck to the wheel rims. Allows easy removal of tyres.
7. **PETROYLE** Upper cylinder lubricant of very high quality containing colloidal graphite.
8. **LINKLYFE** (in liquid form) Has the same unique qualities as solid Linklyfe. Liquid Linklyfe can be brushed on to the chain.
9. **SOLVENT FLUSHING OIL** A powerful flushing oil, contains special additives for the removal of crankcase deposits.
10. **COAXITE** A penetrating fluid for freeing tyres which have stuck to the rims. Harmless to rubber (in handy quart size container).
11. **HYDRAULIC BRAKE FLUID** Suitable for all hydraulic brakes. Boiling point over 500°F. Meets all known specifications including S.A.E. J1703A.
12. **P.D.Q.** (4 oz. tin) A power penetrant for freeing rusted or seized components – Useful workshop pack with flexible spout.
13. **PLUS PENETRATING OIL** A thin searching penetrant containing colloidal graphite for added lubrication.
14. **SPRILLO X** A smooth lubricant designed for the easy fitting of tubeless tyres. Contains no water to cause rim rust or bead rot. Harmless to rubber.
15. **FILTRATE PLUS 20/50** A very high quality multigrade oil containing colloidal graphite.
16. **FILTRATE SUPER 20W/50** A very high quality multigrade oil, suitable for all modern engines. Meets latest specifications.
17. **FILTRATE SUPER LITHIUM GREASE** Suitable for all applications, including water pumps, dynamos, wheel bearings etc.
18. **MULTIGEAR 80/90** Suitable for use as E.P. or Hypoid gear oils.
19. **FILTRATE PLUS 10/30** A very high quality multigrade oil containing colloidal graphite.
20. **FILTRATE LIGHT, MEDIUM and HEAVY GREASES** In useful 7 lb. packs for workshop use. Light Grease suitable for all types of high pressure greasing equipment. Medium Grease for use in hand grease guns. Heavy Grease – a heavy duty grease for screw down cups, etc.
21. **COAXITE** A penetrating fluid which helps free tyres that have stuck to rim (in gallon tin – handy for workshop use).
22. **AUTOMATIC TRANSMISSION FLUID** Fully approved for use in automatic transmissions.
23. **FILTRATE SUPER 20W/50** In handy pint strip top tin.
24. **FILTRATE SUPER LITHIUM** (in handy ¼ lb. packs) Ideal for home or workshop use.
25. **FILTRATE PLUS 2-STROKE OIL** A very high quality 2-Stroke oil containing colloidal graphite.
    FILTRATE SUPER 2 Two stroke oil without colloidal graphite.
26. **FILTRATE BENTONITE GREASE** (in 7 lb. pack) For extremely high temperature applications.
27. **FILTRATE MULTIGEAR 80/90** A multipurpose gear oil (in handy quart pack).
28. **FILTRATE SUPER 10W/30** A high quality multigrade Engine Oil suitable for all modern engines. Meets latest specifications.
29. **FILTRATE SUPER 10W/30** (in handy pint strip top tins).
30. **FILTRATE MOLYTHIUM GREASE** A super lithium grease containing molybdenum disulphide for high temperature, high pressure applications (in 7 lb. Pack).

1. **CRUX** Metallschutzmittel. Rostverhindernd. Feuchtabweisend. Chassisüberzug. Zündungs-Siegelmittel. Akkumulatorkorrosions-Schutzmittel – das Ganze in einer handlichen Aerosolpackung von 425 g.
2. **P.D.Q.** Eine Durchdringflüssigkeit bemerkenswerter Leistung. Hilfreich beim Freimachen zusammengerosteter Teile. – "Pretty Darned Quick" (Blitzschnell) in Packungen von 142 g, mit Aerosol.
3. **PLUSMISCHUNG** Ölzusatzmittel. Enthält ein Konzentrat von Kolloidgraphit – verbessert die Schmierfähigkeit – erleichtert das Einlaufenlassen.
4. **POLYOIL** Ein äusserst nützliches Öl für Haushalt- und Werkstattzwecke.
5. **LINKLYFE** (in fester Form) Ein einzigartiges Kettenschmiermittel, wird nicht abgeschleudert, widerstandsfähig gegen Schmutz und Feuchte. Festes Linklyfe muss zum Eintauchen der Kette erwärmt und als geschmolzenes Linklyfe verwendet werden. Dadurch wird gründliches Eindringen des Schmierstoffs in die Bolzen, Rollen und Platten der Glieder erreicht.
6. **TYREPRIM** Ein Haftverhinderungsmittel welches das Kleben der Reifen an der Radfelge verhütet. Ermöglicht leichtes Abnehmen der Reifen.
7. **PETROYLE** Schmiermittel für den oberen Zylinder, enthält eine beträchtliche Menge Kolloidgraphit.
8. **LINKLYFE** (in flüssiger Form) besitzt die gleichen Eigenschaften, wie festes Linklyfe. Flüssiges Linklyfe kann auf die Kette gepinselt werden.
9. **LÖSLICHES SPÜLÖL** Ein wirksames Spülöl, enthält besondere Zusatzstoffe zum Entfernen von Ablagerungen im Kurbelgehäuse.
10. **COAXITE** Eine Durchdringflüssigkeit zum Freimachen der Reifen, falls sie an der Radfelge kleben. Greift Gummi nicht an (in handlichen Behältern von 1,13 lt. Inhalt).
11. **BREMSHYDRAULIKÖL** Eignet sich für alle hydraulischen Bremssysteme. Siedepunkt über 260°C. Entspricht allen bekannten Vorschriften, einschliesslich SAE 11703A.
12. **P.D.Q.** (113 g Dose) Ein wirksames Mittel zum Freimachen verrosteter oder festgefressener Bestandteile. Zweckdienliche Werkstattpackung mit beweglichem Auslauf.
13. **EINDRINGÖL PLUS** Ein dünnflüssiges forschendes Eindringmittel, enthält zwecks zusätzlicher Schmierung Kolloidgraphit.
14. **SPRILLO X** Ein sanfter Schmierstoff zur Erleichterung der Montage schlauchloser Reifen. Ist wasserfrei, sodass Radfelgen nicht verrosten und Verstärkungswulste nicht zerfallen. Gummi gegenüber unschädlich.
15. **FILTRATE PLUS 20/50** Ein mehrgrädiges Öl sehr hoher Güte, enthält Kolloidgraphit.
16. **FILTRATE SUPER 20W/50** Ein mehrgrädiges Öl sehr hoher Güte, eignet sich für alle modernen Motoren. Entspricht den neuesten Vorschriften.
17. **FILTRATE SUPER LITHIUMFETT** Für alle Anwendungsarten geeignet einschliesslich Wasserpumpen, Dynamos, Radlagerungen, u.s.w.
18. **MULTIGEAR 80/90** Eignet sich zum Gebrauch als E.P.- oder Hypoidgetriebeöl.
19. **FILTRATE PLUS 10/30** Ein mehrgrädiges Öl sehr hoher Güte, enthält Kolloidgraphit.
20. **FILTRATE LEICHT-, MITTEL- und SCHWERFETTE** In zweckdienlichen 3,2 kg Packungen zum Werkstattgebrauch. Leichtfett eignet sich für alle Typen von Hochdruckschmiergeräten, Mittelfett zur Verwendung für Handschmierpistolen, Schwerfett, als hochleistungsfett, für Einschraubnippel u.s.w.
21. **COAXITE** Eine Eindringflüssigkeit zum Freimachen von Reifen, die an Radfelgen festhaften (in 4,5 lit. Dosen zum handlichen Werkstattgebrauch).
22. **ÖL FÜR AUTOMATISCHE ÜBERSETZUNGSGETRIEBE** Zur Verwendung in selbsttätigen Schaltgetrieben voll zugelassen.
23. **FILTRATE SUPER 20W/50** In handlich 0,5 lt. Dosen mit Abreiss-Verschluss.
24. **FILTRATE SUPER LITHIUM** (in handlichen 113 g Packungen) Ideal für Haushalts- und Werkstattzwecke.
25. **FILTRATE PLUS ZWEITAKTÖL** Ein Zweitaktöl sehr hoher Güte enthaltend Kolloidgraphit.
    FILTRATE "SUPER 2" ZWEITAKTÖL Zweitaktöl ohne Kolloid-grafit.
26. **FILTRATE BENTONITFETT** (in 3,2 kg Packungen) Zur Anwendung bei äusserst hohen Temperaturen.
27. **FILTRATE MULTIGEAR 80/90** Ein Mehrzweck-Getriebeöl (in handlichen 1,13 lt. Packungen).
28. **FILTRATE SUPER 10W/30** Ein mehrstufiges Motorenöl hoher Güte. Eignet sich für alle modernen Motoren. Entspricht den neuesten Vorschriften.
29. **FILTRATE SUPER 10W/30** (in handlichen 0,5 lt. Dosen mit Abreissverschluss).
30. **FILTRATE MOLYTHIUMFETT** Ein Superlithiumfett Molybdänbisulfid für hohe Temperaturen, Anwendungen unter hohem Druck (in 3,2 kg Packungen).

1. **CRUX** Protecteur des Métaux – Antirouille – Déplaceur d'humidité – Obturateur des dessous de carrosserie, Obturateur d'allumage, inhibiteur de corrosion des batteries – livré dans un emballage aérosol très maniable de 425 g.
2. **P.D.Q.** Fluide pénétrant de puissance remarquable. Aide à libérer des pièces très rouillées "Pretty Darned Quick" (agissant très rapidement) en emballages aérosols de 142 g.
3. **'PLUS'-COMPOSE** Additif pour huiles – Contient un concentré de graphite colloïdal – améliore la lubrification – facilite le remplissage.
4. **POLYOIL** Huile à usages multiples pour l'entretien ménager et pour atelier.
5. **LINKLYFE** (sous forme solide) Lubrifiant unique pour les chaînes, qui est stable et résiste aux saletés et à l'humidité. Le Linklyfe solide doit être chauffé de façon que la chaîne puisse être immergée dans le Linklyfe fondu; cela assure une pénétration absolue du lubrifiant dans les goupilles, rouleaux et plaques.
6. **TYPEPRIM** Anti-adhésif; empêche les pneus de se coller aux jantes des roues; permet un enlèvement facile des pneus.
7. **PETROYLE** Lubrifiant des hauts de cylindres de très haute qualité contenant du graphite colloïdal.
8. **LINKLYFE** (sous forme liquide) A les mêmes qualités uniques que le Linklyfe solide; il peut être appliqué à la brosse sur la chaîne.
9. **HUILE DE RINCAGE SOLUBLE** Huile de rinçage puissante; contient des additifs spéciaux pour l'enlèvement des dépôts dans le carter.
10. **COAXITE** Fluide pénétrant pour libérer les pneus qui ont collé aux jantes sans danger pour le caoutchouc (en récipients commodes de la taille de 1,13 lit.).
11. **FLUIDE POUR FREINS HYDRAULIQUES** Convient pour tous freins hydrauliques. Point d'ébullition au-dessus de 500°F. (260°C). Répond à toutes spécifications connues, y compris S.A.E. J1703A.
12. **P.D.Q.** (boîtes de 113 g.) Produit pénétrant actif pour libérer les pièces rouillées ou grippées – Emballage utile pour atelier avec ajutage flexible.
13. **HUILE PENETRANTE 'PLUS'** Produit mouillant pénétrant contenant du graphite colloïdal pour augmenter la lubrification.
14. **SPRILLO X** Lubrifiant doux destiné à faciliter le montage des pneus sans chambre à air. Ne contient pas d'eau susceptible de causer la rouille de la jante ou le pourrissement du rebord. Sans danger pour le caoutchouc.
15. **FILTRATE PLUS 20/50** Huile multigrade de très haute qualité contenant du graphite colloïdal.
16. **FILTRATE SUPER 20W/50** Huile multigrade de très haute qualité convenant pour toutes machines modernes. Répond aux toutes dernières spécifications.
17. **GRAISSE A LITHIUM FILTRATE 'SUPER'** Graisse qui convient à toutes les applications, y compris pompes à eau, dynamos, roulements de roues, etc.
18. **MULTIGEAR 80/90** Convient pour utilisation comme huile E.P. ou comme lubrifiant pour engrenages hypoïdes.
19. **FILTRATE PLUS 10/30** Huile multigrade de très haute qualité, contenant du graphite colloïdal.
20. **GRAISSES FILTRATE - LEGERE, MOYENNE ET LOURDE** Graisses en emballages utiles de 3,2 kg. pour utilisation en atelier. Graisse Légère convenable pour tous types d'équipement de graissage sous haute pression. Graisse Moyenne pour utilisation dans les pistolets à graisse manuels. Graisse lourde pour service sévère pour coupelles de vis de réglage, etc.
21. **COAXITE** Fluide pénétrant qui aide à libérer les pneus qui ont collé à la jante (en emballage métallique de 4,545 lt. commode pour utilisation en atelier.
22. **FLUIDE POUR TRANSMISSIONS AUTOMATIQUES** Fluide entièrement approuvé pour utilisation dans les transmissions automatiques.
23. **FILTRATE SUPER 20W/50** En emballages commodes à bouchage métallique de 0,5 lt.
24. **FILTRATE SUPER LITHIUM** En emballages commodes de 113 g. appropriés pour usage domestique aussi bien qu'à l'atelier.
25. **HUILE DEUX-TEMPS FILTRATE 'PLUS'** Huile de très haute qualité pour moteurs deux temps; contenant du graphite colloïdal.
    HUILE DEUX-TEMPS FILTRATE 'SUPER 2' Huile deux temps sans de graphite colloïdal.
26. **GRAISSE BENTONITE FILTRATE** Graisse Bentonite (en emballages de 3,2 kg.) pour applications en températures extrêmement élevées.
27. **FILTRATE MULTIGEAR 80/90** Huile pour engrenages à usages multiples (en emballages commodes de 1,13 lit.).
28. **FILTRATE SUPER 10W/30** Huile multigrade de haute qualité pour moteurs convenant pour tous moteurs modernes; répond aux toutes dernières spécifications.
29. **FILTRATE SUPER 10W/30** (en emballages commodes de 0,5 lt. à bouchage métallique).
30. **GRAISSE FILTRATE 'MOLYTHIUM'** Graisse supérieure au lithium contenant du bisulfure de molybdène pour applications à haute température et à hautes pressions (en emballages de 3,2 kg.).

The **plus** range

Oil film only gives protection if it is thick enough to prevent moving parts touching. In practice this is not always the case. For example, during running-in relatively large irregularities usually pierce the oil film and when there is accidental loss of oil pressure or tearing the same thing occurs, and again when the temperature is raised ordinary additives eventually lose their effectiveness. Filtrate Plus is insoluble in all of these circumstances, because it bonds firmly to the rubbing surfaces, has a low shear strength and thus prevents metal-to-metal contact and wear. The adhesion of Graphite — the "Plus" in Filtrate Plus — to metal surfaces is such that effective lubrication can be maintained at temperatures considerably above those at which oil becomes ineffective. Filtrate Plus combines the best qualities of the finest lubricating oils plus the protection of the finest solid lubricant. This is PLUS advantage.

FILTRATE PLUS 10/30
A very high quality
multigrade oil containing
colloidal graphite.

FILTRATE PLUS 20/50
A very high quality
multigrade oil containing
colloidal graphite.

RATE PLUS
ROKE OIL A very
quality 2-Stroke oil
aining colloidal
tite.

RATE SUPER 2
stroke oil without
idal graphite.

PLUS COMPOUND OR
additive. Contains a
concentrate of colloidal
graphite — improves
lubrication — eases
running-in.

PETROYLE Upper
cylinder lubricant of very
high quality containing
colloidal graphite

PLUS PENETRATING
OIL. A thin searching
penetrant containing
colloidal graphite for
added lubrication.

FILTRATE PRODUCT BULLETIN | No. 21a.

FILTRATE

2/Stroke

PLUS 2/Stroke   The "plus" in Filtrate products indicates the incorporation of colloidal graphite. Colloidal graphite consists of microscopically small (40 millionths of an inch) plates of dry lubricant which cling to metal but repel one another, thus maintaining permanent suspension in the lubricant as well as preventing build-up on bearing surfaces. The graphoid surface, once established, will provide lubrication even when the oil film is temporarily disrupted and at temperatures up to 600 °C.

SUPER 2   This is a top-grade two-stroke lubricant containing the latest developments in additives designed to prevent plug-whiskering and reduce port deposits. Super 2 falls within the SAE 30 classification, and is basically Plus 2 Stroke without the "plus." This grade is marketed to suit those users who do not like the black colour of "Plus", and to meet the requirements of certain engine manufacturers who do not permit the inclusion of graphite in their approved lubricants.

Plus 2 Stroke is officially approved by:— B.S.A., TRIUMPH, LAMBRETTA, GREEVES, YAMAHA & JAWA. C.Z.

Super 2 is officially approved by PUCH

FILTRATE LTD., FILTRATE WORKS, LEEDS LS1 1LS. Tel. 357755

Courtesy of Filtrate Oils.

FILTRATE OILS

Filtrate oils were the oldest independent oil company in the world until it was taken over in the late 1980s, or early 1990s, by a company called Hunter. Filtrate oils were no longer produced.

Filtrate started up in 1807. Their oil was then produced by crushing beans and supplied oils for Stephens' Rocket and most steam engines at that time. Oil was supplied for industrial and agriculture use.

Filtrate produced racing oils for some Honda and Motoguzzi racing in the IOM with great success and supported Barry Bowles to win back the Land Speed Records.

Fletchers School of Motoring in Swansea was reckoned to be the second oldest driving school in the world. One of their Mini vehicles completed 176,000 miles on Filtrate 30 Oil on the same engine.

As I have said before, they made the best two stroke oil along with many other top class products.

Club run to Newhaven showing off our new TV 175 Series III. Our first club outing with our new scooter.

LAMBRETTA DEALER SERVICE WEEKS.

lambretta

SERVICE AGENT

SERVICE REPORT

Date .... Owner .... Address ....
Mileage .... Model .... Engine No. .... Reg No. ....

UNIT	ITEM CHECKED	✓=OK	REMARKS	UNIT	ITEM CHECKED	✓=OK	REMARKS
ENGINE	Mountings / Bevel gears / Ignition system / Kick starter / Carburettor / Fuel pipe / Exhaust system / Oil leaks / Compression			BRAKES	Front linings / Rear linings / Front cable / Rear cable / Pivots / Cable clamps		
				FRONT SUSPENSION	Springs / Hub bearings / Shock absorbers		
CLUTCH	Operation / Pull-rod adjustment / Cable adjustment			REAR SUSPENSION	Torsion bar setting / Shock absorber		
GEARBOX	Action / Oil level and leaks / Gear cable adjustments			INSTRUMENTS	Speedometer		
REAR AXLE	Bearings / Bevel gears / Oil level and leaks			ELECTRICAL	Battery / Wiring (visible) / Lamps / Horn / Starter LDA only		
WHEELS and TYRES	Wheels and nuts / Spare wheel / Tyre condition, front / Tyre condition, rear / Tyre pressures			REMARKS			
STEERING	Head bearings / Links / Alignment						

If as a result of the inspection of your Lambretta, it is shown that certain items are not satisfactory, you are strongly recommended that they should be attended to with:

IMPORTANT. The examination of the above machine by a member of our staff and the completion of this report does not in any way constitute liability by Lambretta Concessionaires Limited for the machine or any of its component parts.

Courtesy of Mrs Edna Calder — Director of Lambretta Concessionaires

As a dealer, if the firm wanted to run a service week, then a good workshop and special tools to do the job were required. The firm had to advertise in their local papers to let people know what they were doing and book appointments for a free service check-up.

Lambretta Concessionaires Limited would also back the dealer by providing free banners and posters, and send the dealer technical staff to carry out the safety checks on all the scooters booked in. The dealer had to provide tea/coffee/buns in the hope they would get a lot of work and possibly new sales from the hard work completed during service week.

LAMBRETTA SERVICE DEPARTMENT

I modified the layout of our service department stores to cut down waiting time for spare parts. All spares had a part number from the main store. We laid our parts out in order of use and in some cases a special number was given; for example, Steering Bearings are in six parts all with their own part number. We used the part number on the large bottom frame cone 19061023 and added a 'K' to the end of the part number, which stood for a complete kit of steering bearings. We did this on many items to cut down the time spent waiting for spares.

I was required to complete engine strip downs for the motorcycle magazines and at motorcycle shows for the public. I was also sent out on 'Dealer Service Weeks'.

As I had a scooter, I was asked to 'run-in' all the new models as they came out for the motorcycle magazines, to road test them. What a job! It seemed to me as if I was always riding a new scooter. My neighbours must have thought I had pots of money.

I spent many hours helping, with the aid of Vern, to comprise a trade repair time on all jobs. The way we set about this was to take one of our demo scooters and strip it down and then refit the parts.

A frame change for LDB scooters was 23 hours and 21 hours for LI Series I and II scooters, down to 17 hours. For Series III and GP scooters, I only managed to do a frame and fork change in 12 hours once on a crash repair job. It was calculated that if I took one hour to complete a job that would become two hours to allow for rusted parts. Further time was also allowed to remove accessories to carry out the work. This was done to help dealers with the costing of repairs.

From time to time, we had young lads come to work in the service department for one or two weeks to gain some experience on Lambretta servicing and repair work before going to work for a dealer.

TRADE WORKSHOP TIMES

Listed below are samples of times for single repair jobs. With regard to the brakes, the time allowed also included washing the wheels and drums. The engine and frame were also washed on the 3,000 service. Any extra work carried out would have time added to the times shown below:

Change handlebars 2¼ hours

Frame change — GP & SX 17 hours. LI I & II 21 hours. LDB 23 hours.

Forks change — 2½ hours.

Steering bearing change — 1¾ hours.

Replace one gear cable — 1 hour; two gear cables — 1½ hours.

Replace clutch plates — 1½ hours.

Replace rear and front brake shoes — 2 hours.

Service and replace front disc pads — 1¾ hours.

Replace front wheel bearings and oil seals — 1½ hours.

Fit modified kick-start shaft — 1½ hours.

Fit new engine mount — 1 hour.

3,000 mile service — 5 hours.

Engine overhaul — 5½ hours.

Engine decoke — 3½ hours.

Barrel and piston — 2½ hours.

When re-building the front forks, we always greased the fork link bolts on all the later models with nylon bushes to stop the bolt seizing in the metal sleeve. Grease was applied to the four washers at the side of the links to stop water penetration to the bolt. On the rear brake pedal, we re-fitted the old type brass bush with lots of grease to cut down the sideways movement of the pedal. Some dealers would send the scooters to us to repair and would put their mark up on the price of the repair to the customer. Occasionally, a problem could not be solved, so again it would be sent to us to sort out. Once done, the scooter would be sent back to the dealer. This was good for all of us working in the service department, as it broke up the day-to-day routine work.

SOUTHAMPTON RALLY MAY 1966

A very good GT 200 Lambretta scooter with converted handlebars to make room for the twin headlamps. The lad with the fag was the owner. The GT 200 Lambretta also has spot lights attached to the front forks. He must have just ridden it in a straight line. He also has one of the sports silencers with twin pipes one each side of the scooter. I think this one has a

bracket fixed to the rear of the frame. The early ones had a special nut that replaced the standard hub nut; it had a sealed bearing attached with a bracket round the outer part of the bearing, then by an arm to the tail pipe. The bearing became very hot and soon failed, ripping the tail pipe out of the silencer smashing into the side panel and footboard in the process.

CROYDON, SURREY RODEO 1966

The Croydon Rodeo was a very good rally for us as it was only a few miles away from where we lived.

Members of our club in fancy dress at the dance.

Peter Simmonds with his Concord D'Elegance scooter, to which he won 1st prize in his class.

Croydon Rodeo 1966 Jan and Dick Sedgley with bambino Stephanie.

We were told we could not enter the fancy dress competition as our costumes were shop bought, which was not true, as we had made these outfits way back in the 1950s for the rakes rally.

We won best new buggy; not sure if was for my scooter or our little bambino.

MALLORY PARK ECONOMY RUN

Here we are again, scrutineering check over and petrol drained, one gallon of fuel refilled in the tank, and sealed up. Scooters were parked in a bay so no competitors could go near them until ready to go on the track. Your speedo was set so the competitor would know how many miles were completed on the gallon of fuel. I was not looking forward to another four more hours without stopping.

This time I did a lot better on the MPG, but only came second as the 150 specials were in the same class as the TV 175 scooters.

The reason given for this was the 150 special scooter had the same size carburettor as the 175 scooter, no comment by a very miffed me at the time. The 175 scooter was being dropped in the UK so all the article publicity from now on would be on the 125/150 and 200 models. Certificates were only given to the winners this time round. This could be the first sign of Lambretta Concessionaires Limited cutting back on expenses for LCGB.

John Wood of the Epsom Scooter Club won the 200 class with 119 miles to the gallon.

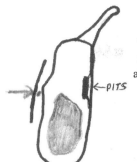

The circuit where Dave Cox wrote my SX 200 off, racing in the Special Class, round about where the * is. My attempt at drawing the map of Mallory Park Circuit, from memory, and not to scale.

←—PITS

ISLE OF MAN DISASTER 1966

A shipping strike closed the Isle of Man scooter week, which must have caused a huge problem for the people involved with the scooter week, including all the scooterists due to take part. This resulted in a huge loss of income for the island.

The concessionaires had prepared three 125 or 150 specials for the event. The scooters were completely striped down. All the handlebar controls were cleaned and polished and refitted. All cables inners were checked and oiled, both brakes were removed and cleaned. Cams and pivots greased before refitting the shoes. The engines were completely stripped down, all barrels, pistons and gears were crack tested. All other parts checked before refitting. All the studs in the crank cases were removed and tapex inserts fitted, before refitting the studs. These inserts were also fitted to the lower handlebars to strengthen the supports for the gear and throttle rods. This work was carried out to try and prevent the scooters having a problem if they were involved in an accident. They were also fitted with Avon cling tyres, as they performed the best in wet conditions. My only involvement with these scooters was to make the twelve volt battery conversion kits for them. All this work carried out was to no avail in the end, because of the seaman's strike. Whoever landed up with these scooters were very lucky indeed.

LAMBRETTA CONCESSIONAIRES MOVES INTO THE MOTORCYCLE MARKET.

Lambretta Concessionaires took over Suzuki motorcycles for the UK market. Along with all the spares and accessories, they also had some very useful tools for the workshop and a little 50cc racing motorcycle which everybody in the workshop had a go on. The last thing in this collection was a black velo solex cycle/moped. The 39cc engine was mounted over the front wheel, which wore out the front tyre quite quickly. I believe this was a French moped! You could say Lambretta's 3rd moped once they were all sold to the trade; no further orders for this little moped were placed.

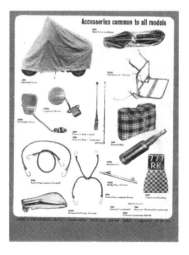

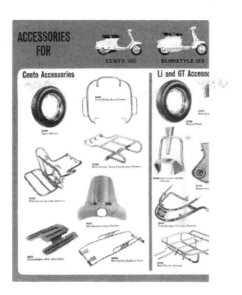

Courtesy of Mrs Edna Calder — Director of Lambretta
Concessionaires.

185

A fine example of what the GT Lambretta stood for, speed and endurance without falling apart. Many of the faults mentioned on Lambretta scooters over the years was lack of proper servicing and poor maintenance.

CHAPTER 8
THE SMARTEST SCOOTER YET.

Courtesy of Morton Media.

Courtesy of Morton Media.

Model changes GT 200 SX 200

It had been reported incorrectly in some motorcycle magazines, that the GT 200 was a bored out 175. In fact, it had a much larger opening in the new crankcase to take the 200 barrel and piston; plus cylinder head and crankshaft, and a complete set of gears. The silencer looked the same, but was different inside to the TV 175 type.

The report may have come about because the first TV 200 engine was fitted into an old 175 Series II scooter, this was just for a test assessment by the Concessionaires Limited at Croydon, Surrey and probably where the mix up came about. The road test was done by the late Brian Gibbs, who was no light weight, but managed to get a speedo reading of well over 70 mph. Everybody who rode it was 'over the moon' with its performance, apart from the 175 II drum brake of course. All production 200 models had disc brakes.

Anybody who had one of the first batches of 200's had the fastest standard Lambretta ever. A few of these were on the Lambretta demo fleet. After that, the barrel ports were changed to cut down the speed a little. I was always on the lookout for the special identification mark on the first barrels which were so good.

The SX 200 was a better model than the GT 200 in looks, but not so much in performance. Most of the troubles had been ironed out. There was not so much vibration and because of the lower gears and lower compression ratio, it was better in traffic and around town. The top speed was not as high as the GT, though the engineers from Innocenti disagreed.

There was a meeting at Croydon Airport with some of the engineers on the SX's, against our Demo GT 200 ridden by Brian Gibbs and Vern Laville. The result, no contest; the GT came out top every time, whoever rode it.

Having said that, the SX was a decent scooter to ride. It looked very good when Lambretta Concessionaires Limited put some colour on the panels, as with the GT they came to the UK all white. The SX 200, however, was not without trouble; the con rod was very light in weight and had a lot of end float at the crankpin end. At the small end, you had two piston shims; these were added to cut down on the piston clank in the barrel, along with a lower compression ratio. Unfortunately, the conrod sheared near the small end and the conrod wrapped itself round the big end, which caused some damage to the crank case and barrel. This was rectified by modifying the crank.

Spare Part Changes

There were at least four Series III type silencers. First one was for 125/150/175 with a thin main fixing bracket, also the GT 200 type, with a thin main fixing bracket. Next was the SX 200 type with an extra fixing bracket to the crankcase plus a double thickness main fixing bracket. There was also the 125/150 specials and SX 150 silencers with different tail pipes and fixing brackets to the crankcase under the box. In the end, there was just one box to fit all models, including all GP models.

SX 200 - 1966

When the SX 200 came out we had to run-in five or six scooters as soon as possible. The service manager, Vern and I did most of the riding due to the weather conditions. Three other people helped occasionally.

Courtesy of Mrs Edna Calder — Director of Lambretta Concessionaires.

The scooters were all white. The two-tone colours were completed in the spray shop at Croydon, Surrey.

Lambretta Concessionaires always produced special colour for the motorcycle shows. On one occasion, right at the last minute, metal flake colours were used which caused a problem when refitting the horncasting. We had to fit washers behind the leg shield fixing brackets as the handlebars were rubbing on the top of the horncasting, because the metal flake, plus several coats of lacquer, made them much thicker. All the horncastings had to be resprayed; I had to refit them with the lacquer still soft. I was called a 'coppers delight' as you could just see my very fine hand prints in the lacquer. They were polished out once the scooters were on the stand. This was just a small part of the stress and strains of attending motorcycle shows, but I loved every minute of it. Talking to people who liked the scooters you were showing, listening to what they had to say, and sharing my knowledge of Lambretta Scooters with them. Also being helpful if they had a problem such as bad servicing by dealers and no guarantee if they had pattern parts fitted. There were a few argument to spice thing up a bit. All part of the job.

I had my SX 200 re-sprayed lemon, black and white. Everybody took the mickey out of my colour scheme. Sometime later, Lambretta Concessionaires Limited bought out a similar colour scheme on the latest SX 200's. So it appeared I had not picked a bad colour scheme after all!

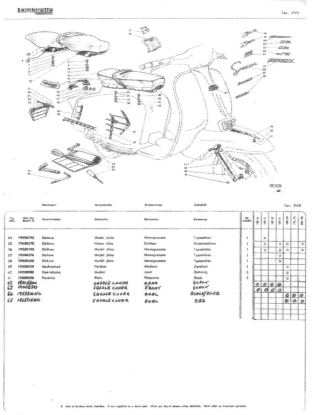

N. Rif.	Cod. No. Bestell N.	Descrizione	Description	Désignation	Benennung	Qt. Anzahl								
54	19490190	Distivo	Model plate	Monogramme	Typschilchen	1		o						
55	19658170	Distivo	Nome ciclo	Ecriteau	Firmenschilchen	1			o	o	o		o	
56	19550136	Distivo	Model plate	Monogramme	Typschilchen	1			o	o	o		o	
57	19656170	Distivo	Model plate	Monogramme	Typschilchen	1				o				
58	19858160	Distivo	Model plate	Monogramme	Typschilchen	1				o				
59	19250540	Moduletura	Finisher	Moulure	Zierstück	1					o			
60	19258965	Guarnizione	Gasket	Joint	Dichtung	2					o			
61	19080090	Mostrina	Plate	Plaquette	Blech	2					o			
62	19855500	SADDLE CLOTH	REAR		BZRAZ			o	o	o				
63	19405500	SADDLE COVER	FRONT		GREEN			o	o	o				
64	19655160	SADDLE COVER	DUAL		BLACK/BLUE							o	o	o
65	19655160	SADDLE COVER	DUAL		RED							o	o	o

Accessori	Accesorios	Accessories	Zubehör

The leaflet above is of the latest parts book that covers seven models for the UK market. At a glance, you can see what parts went on each model on original production from Innocenti for the English market. Some additions were added as shown in the parts book above. There were two other colours of dual seat covers, green and light blue, not shown on the list above as at that time they did not have a part number. I think the part numbers would carry on from the last one shown so would be 19655160 scooter cover green, and 19655170 scooter cover light blue.

LAMBRETTINO MOPED — 1966

The Lambrettino moped had a production run of about one year and in that time, about 15,000/16,000 rolled off the line. It had a 39cc engine single speed centrifugal clutch and was olive green in colour. The petrol tank, engine covers, headlamp and tool roll box were all made in plastic. Unfortunately, this moped suffered with a few problems with the magneto and clutch.

Some of the mopeds were already at the dealers and on the road with customers before the faults came to light. All machines had to be recalled for modification. An engineer was sent from Innocenti to help out; unfortunately, I cannot remember his name, but I do remember I called him 'Not Possible'. If anything went wrong, up would go his arms and he would say "This is not possible." He was a very good person and I got on very well with him. My biggest regret was I did not speak Italian.

I worked with him for three or four weeks until all the modifications were completed. Rex White also helped from time to time. The magneto had an internal HT and LT coil combined, which failed. A new LT coil had to be fitted to the stator plate. A new HT coil had to be fitted to a bracket that was welded to the frame. This was situated under the plastic cover on top of the frame above the engine.

The trouble with the centrifugal clutch was oil travelling into the drum and onto the shoes, through the threaded spindle to the drum, and ran on and through the two holes in the back of the drum. The holes were there for the tool to undo the drum. A new way had to be found to undo this, as the new drum had the holes filled in to keep the oil out to stop the oil travelling along the thread. An 'O' ring was fitted; all oil removed from the spindle and a blue Hylomar gasket compound was applied. This was the only time we were allowed to use a gasket compound. After that, all was well and off they went to the dealer.

The SX model was a 50cc and had a variable speed transmission which gave it a bit more speed, but was more expensive. I do not think Lambretta Concessionaires Limited took up this model for sale in the United Kingdom.

I believe this was the only colour sold in the United Kingdom.

OLIVE GREEN LAMBRETTINO

Brands Hatch 1967

I believe, the first high speed trial race at Brands Hatch was in December 1966. We had three club members competing. It was a very cold and wet day so it was no surprise that a lot of people came off their scooters or broke down. The three competitors from our club were victims, not a good result this time.

I had always been happy to look after the scooters, but now thought I could do better. At the ripe old age of 25, I started out taking part in competitions. The second Brands Hatch event soon came around and I was in the 175 class, and again it was wet and cold. At the time I thought, 'what am I doing here'.

The ride down to Brands Hatch was very cold and when we saw the track, we did not think we would be racing as there was frost on the surface in places. Several cars were allowed to drive around the track for a few laps to test out the grip, which was found to be OK. The scooters were checked and it was time for our practice laps

to see how we coped with the times set for each lap. I was put in with the 200 class, but would be timed in my 175 class.

Off we went in the wet and all too soon our time was up, and out came the sun. The track started to dry out, and as luck would have it, off went the 175 classes. I did not expect to be in with a chance.

To say I was surprised to hear my name called out for first place was an understatement indeed. So, I caught the bug and carried on for about seven years with some success over that time. I was very pleased to receive this cup.

DECEMBER 1967 RAY COLLINS MEMORIAL SCRAMBLE MEETING AT BRANDS HATCH 1967

Courtesy of Peter Lumley. Dick at Brands Hatch.

(Left) One of the junior heats gets away. John Cooper (on extreme right) is only able to operate his first gear. (Below) The Ray Collins Memorial Scramble final gets under way. Two standard machines in the line-up are ridden by P Bullock (66) and J. Foster (73).

Many thanks to Peter Lumley, Editor of Scootering & Three Wheeler for permission this report and pictures for the 1967.

Back again at Brands Hatch this time on the motorcycle scramble track. To say it was cold, wet and muddy would not be an understatement. Somehow I got through the heats into the new comers final. I am Number 60 in the line-up. I was not very near the front at the finish, but I did enjoy myself.

I sold this scooter soon after this event as an old football injury to my knee started to give me a lot of pain.

A SEARCH FOR MORE IMPROVEMENTS

Lambretta Concessionaires Limited was always looking at new products and projects. One of these being proper fuel injection, not drip feed like the Wal Phillips type for the Lambretta. It was too complicated and would have cost too much, so Lambretta Concessionaires Limited dropped the project.

Another project that was considered was a five speed gearbox conversion, long before Roy's of Hornchurch made them. It would have meant a new longer lay shaft, a new back plate, front sprocket sleeve, chain guides, clutch cover, gear selector, gear group plus sorting out the five gears plus handlebar gear control. Once again, the cost would be too high, so this was also dropped.

Lambretta Concessionaires Limited also re-exported quite a few Centos' in kit form. We had to take the wheels off, take out the forks, and remove the saddle and the handlebars which stayed attached to the cables, and remove the headlamp. All the nuts, bolts, screws, were put in a bag, and put in the plastic toolbox and finally a crate had to be made up. I am not sure where they were sent, possibly to Ireland.

We also had 2 or 3 little J 50cc models all in white sent over from Innocenti, but they were too slow for our roads. Also, the lights were not up to UK standard and there was no stop light, speedo or number plate bracket.

It was about this time that the so called LI Series IV made an appearance. When one turned up in the workshop, my thoughts were that Innocenti were using up all their old spare parts stock. They could also have been put together for a cheap export order that may have been cancelled. It could tie in perhaps, with the order Lambretta Concessionaires Limited at Croydon received for the Cento's for re-export in kit form possibly to Ireland.

A FLI175

Lambretta Concessionaires Limited sprayed one of these in orange and it was sign written for the company that sold Bazooka Bubble Gum.

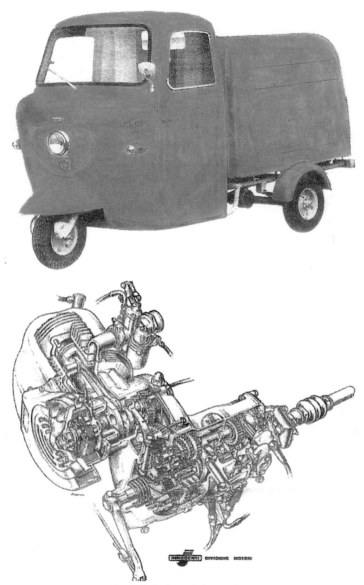

Exploded view of the engine.

FLI 175 THREE WHEELER VAN

Apart from routine work and servicing day after day, it was a challenge to get something different to work on, like a three wheeler van. It was a FLI 175 with a clutch problem. When first gear was selected it would jump forward, which was not good if you were in heavy traffic. We found there was too much oil in the gearbox and the trouble was the oil was surging over the clutch bell, filling the gap between the plates and was forcing the top plate past the clutch bell. This was modified and oil level lowered, which solved the problem.

On later models, the cork clutch plates were replaced with phosphor bronze ones and an additional centre clutch spring fitted. On the hand pull starter models, care had to be taken holding the handle the correct way as you could rap your knuckles on the floor if the machine misfired on starting up.

LAMBRETTA CONCESSIONAIRES LIMITED SIDE-CAR FITTING

If a side car was to be fitted to your Lambretta, the first thing to do was remove the leg shields then make a template out of sheet metal or plywood and drill four holes to line up with the holes in the frame struts. This was done so welding the frame struts back would be level and in the right place when refitting the leg shields. Then the two front struts were cut off, taking care not to cut into the main frame tube and clean off any weld that was left on the main frame. The left-hand strut was welded back to the right-hand side of the frame, and the right-hand strut welded to the left-hand side. This was done to make room for the side-car bracket. Finally, making sure you bolted the strut to the template before welding it back to the frame.

Next, you had to drill two holes for the stop light switch. On some makes of the side-cars, they had a brake fitted so you would have had to drill through the rear frame strut to fit the cable and cable stop, and then attach to the rear brake pedal.

To fit the side-car chassis to the frame, you had to ensure you did not over tighten the bracket at this stage. If you had the flange type chassis, you made sure all the rubbers were in good condition, then bolted them up very tight. You were then able to align the sidecar wheel. This must toe in 1½". Metal bars were best for this job; one kept the scooter wheels in line; the other on the outside of the side-car wheel. A tape measure was used to ensure you had the right amount of toe in, at the same time ensuring the side-car was level. Finally, the nuts and bolts were tightened. The next job was to make sure the scooter leaned out away from the side-car. The best way was to run a plumb line down the centre of the scooter. The headlamp bulb needed be to the left of the plumb line. This was done to stop the outfit diving to the left because of the camber of the road. The next step was to tighten up the clamp bolts round the frame; and test ride the scooter. Finally, you needed to refit the leg shields and horn casting, then the side-car body and connect up the lights.

A lot of people lent the scooter into the side-car because they felt safer that way, but you needed a strong left arm to hold the scooter in a straight line. The rear brake pedal was also modified to take the side-car brake cable and of course we had to extend the loom for the lights on the side-car. The tyre pressures were 25 lbs on all three wheels on the box side-cars.

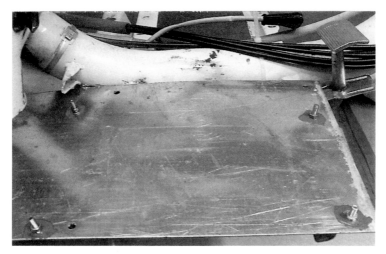

The template bolted to the frame struts before cutting off the front strut.

The S strut marked in red before cutting off. Then fitted around the other way so the S would then face backwards.

These members of the Epsom Lambretta Club choose to ride on Michelin ACS scooter tyres

These are their reasons why

About the Club

The Epsom Lambretta Club—the Whirlwinds—was formed in 1958 and is affiliated to the Lambretta Club of Great Britain and to the Scooter Association (London area). Sunday runs, camping week-ends, dances and a unique winter game of five-a-side football make up some of the club's activities. Members also compete regularly in economy runs, scrambles and high-speed trials—with some success, too. Last year club member John Wood won the Mallory Park Economy Run (200 class), and club secretary Dick Sedgeley took first place in the 1965 Economy Run at Brands (175 class).

"I'm a scooter mechanic and I've always used ACS because they're better for mileage and grip".

"They don't slide in the wet and they don't pick up stones as much as other tyres".

"Their road-holding and wear is better than other tyres and they give me extra miles to the gallon".

"ACS wear better and give a better back grip in the wet than any other tyre I've tried".

MICHELIN

67/28/G8

Epsom Lambretta Club were asked to take part in this Michelin scooter advert because most of our members were seen riding with their tyres at scooter events. I used Michelin tyres on a 12 hour race meeting with great success in very cold and wet conditions. An advert full of information. I still use Michelin tyres today.

MORECOMBE/MATLOCK RALLY AUG/SEPT 1967

About ten club members attended the rally. Some members entered into the fields events. Jan and I went by car with 2 year old Stephanie and six-week-old baby Debbie and stayed in Morecambe for a week. Everyone had a great time although the weather was not so good.

A new SX 150 one of many new scooters I luckily was able to run-in for Lambretta Concessionaires Limited before going out for Road Test by Motorcycle Magazines.

Little Stephanie in a helmet much too big for her head, in our back garden at Tudor Drive, Morden, Surrey.

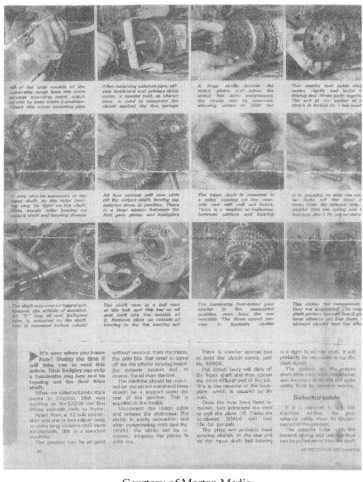

Courtesy of Morton Media.

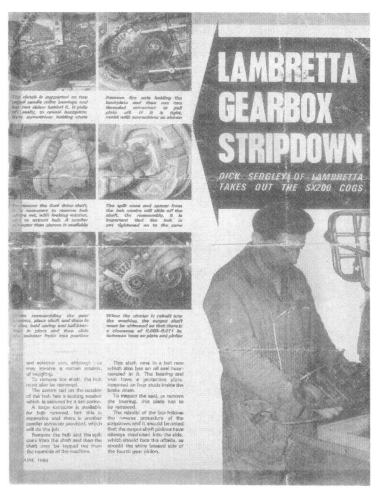

Courtesy of Morton Media.

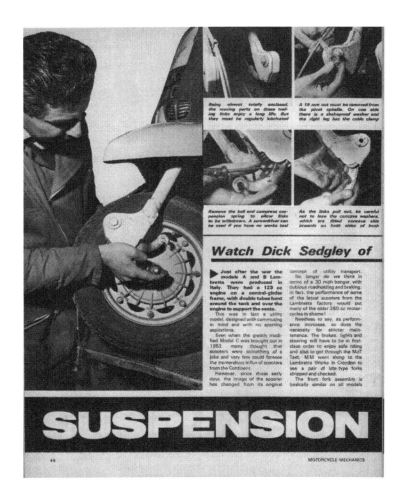

After starting the pivot spindle with a soft-ended hammer, it can be driven from the leg with a thin drift. If tight, support fork

Spring rebound buffers should be removed before the trailing links. Prise them out with a screwdriver. Old type had two locating screws

Here you can see the difference between the old and new rebound buffers. The later type simply push in the bottom leg cover

Bushes should be removed as soon as play becomes noticeable. This point indicated is where they tend to seize on the spindle

The picture shows trailing link with nylon bush inside, the pin on which the link pivots and the two metal concave washers

Piston and spring slide out together, once the link is out of the way. Turning the piston while in fork will test its straightness

Spring wear is negligible, but if you own a 'vintage' Lambretta, you can check the free length of the spring against a new one

Another way to check the piston for straightness is by holding a rule or other perfectly straight piece of metal alongside it

Lambretta strip and check the front forks

and requires little attention except for monthly lubrication.

Dismantling is fairly straight-forward. After detaching the brake cable from the wheel, un-screwing the speedometer drive and detaching the drive-box, the wheel can be removed.

Before commencing the strip, it makes the work a lot more pleasant if the forks are washed down in petrol and it often pays to saturate the pivot nuts in penetrating oil and leave them for half an hour or so to allow it to do its work.

On this particular strip, we did not remove the forks from the frame, although this might be necessary if the pivot spindles are very tight in their location.

With a 19 mm spanner the nut

on the pivot pin can be undone and the spindle freed off and knocked out with a thin-ended punch.

If excessive force is needed to drive out the spindle, be sure to hold something behind the fork leg to give it some support, or the leg itself will become damaged.

Buffers

With the spindles removed, the rubber rebound buffers for the suspension springs can be prised out.

On earlier models there is a plate on the buffer and two fixing screws must be removed, along with the grease nipple under the lever before it will come out. But on the latest forks the plate has

been discarded and the buffer is simply a solid block of rubber.

In order to withdraw the trailing links, the suspension springs must be compressed. This can be done very easily with the special service tool, or by inserting a lever under the piston which guides the spring.

The springs, pistons and piston guide rings can now be pulled from the legs.

The TV 175 has an external shock absorber which should last for an indefinite period. However, if it does lose its efficiency after a considerable mileage, a factory replacement unit will have to be bought.

Examine the ball and the cups in piston and, and trailing link, make sure the whole assembly is

cleaned and greased before rebuilding.

Following a tumble, be sure that forks are not bent and the trailing links are not damaged.

Haphazard straightening is a dangerous occupation. If you are not sure about anything, don't take chances—ask a Lambretta dealer, he'll be able to supply replacement parts or do any straightening which may be necessary—and do it safely!

If lubricated regularly, these forks can go for great mileages with very little wear and bushes etc., are cheap and easy to replace.

Lightly grease all moving parts before reassembling—not for-getting the nylon bushes in the link pivots.

OVERHAUL

MARCH 1969

47

Courtesy of Bauer Archives.

209

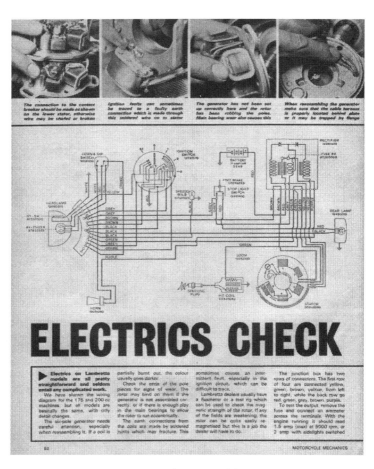

ELECTRICS CHECK

Electrics on Lambretta models are all pretty straightforward and seldom entail any complicated work.

We have shown the wiring diagram for the 175 and 200 cc machines, but all models are basically the same, with only detail changes.

The six-pole generator needs careful attention, especially when reassembling it. If a coil is partially burnt out, the colour usually goes darker.

Check the ends of the pole pieces for signs of wear. The rotor may bind on them if the generator is not assembled correctly, or if there is enough play in the main bearings to allow the rotor to run eccentrically.

The earth connections from the coils are made by soldered joints which may fracture. This sometimes causes an intermittent fault, especially in the ignition circuit, which can be difficult to trace.

Lambretta dealers usually have a fluxmeter or a test rig which can be used to check the magnetic strength of the rotor. If any of the fields are weakening, the rotor can be quite easily re-magnetised but this is a job the dealer will have to do.

The junction box has two rows of connectors. The first row of four are connected yellow, green, brown, yellow, from left to right, while the back row go red, green, grey, brown, purple.

To test the output, remove the fuse and connect an ammeter across the terminals. With the engine running it should read 1.5 amp (max) at 5000 rpm, or 2 amp with sidelights switched.

82   MOTORCYCLE MECHANICS

Courtesy of Bauer Archives.

Courtesy of Bauer Archives.

211

EPSOM WHIRLWINDS SCOOTER CLUB

Our scooter club was always, in the main, a social club. We did attend some road trials; luckily when we started to enter track events, it did not break the club in two which did happen to some clubs.

We had an Epsom Whirlwind patch made up for our overalls, when taking part in field events.

Shown below is the L.C.G.B. Championship table as at February 1st 1968. At the time, I believe, I was the only one taking part in track events. Other members listed below then took up the challenge. Ray Sweeney and Peter Simmons started it off way back in 1966. I started competitions in 1967 along with John Wood, and then Paul Gilbert, Bill Brunning, Tony Pawsey, Andy Pink, Jim Issard and Dave Cox. Apologies if I have left anybody out!

THE CHAMPIONSHIP TABLE

Points and Positions as at February 1st

	Champion Clubman		points		Champion Club	points
1st	G. Pearce	Bromley	90	1st	Bromley 'Innocents'	329
2nd	N. Frost	Bromley	77	2nd	Watford	194
2nd	C. Tomlin	Bromley	77	3rd	Purley 'Lions'	183
4th	R. Willett	Purley	76	4th	Luton	117
5th	R. Sedgley	Epsom	75	5th	Epping 'Rakes'	103
5th	N. Barnes	Watford	75	6th	Vagabonds	99
7th	B. C. Hull	Bromley	66	7th	Epsom 'Whirlwinds'	78
7th	C. D. Armett	Purley	66	8th	L.C. London 'Jet Set'	70
7th	K. Webb	Bromley	66	9th	Surbiton	50
7th	M. Collins	L.C. London	66	10th	Grantham 'Newtonians'	45
7th	P. Mullinder	Luton	66	11th	Leicester 'Reynards'	37
12th	K. Raynsford	Bromley	65	12th	Birmingham 'Cherubs'	35
13th	P. Russell	Watford	61	12th	Wessex	35
14th	E. West	Watford	58	14th	Leicester Sporting	34
15th	T. McGee	Epping	57	15th	Bristol 'Neptunes'	30

CADWELL PARK, LINCOLNSHIRE, HIGH SPEED TRIALS 1968

I competed in three events at Cadwell Park; two events were on the full circuit and one on the short circuit. I believe Paul Gilbert and I were the only two club members from our club competing on the track at this time. Other club members took up the challenge with us in the next couple of years.

Cadwell Park was a fantastic circuit for scooters and motorbikes. The race was nearly called off because the track was water logged in one area. In the end, the rain let up and we got the green light to race.

It was also my best result of the three times I raced here. I came third to which I was very happy with as I was on my TV 175 Series III in the 200 class.

The other two races at Cadwell Park I came either fourth, fifth or sixth. In fact, I never came lower than sixth in any road race I took part in, apart from falling off twice at Lydden Hill and an engine blow up at Snetterton. To gain that first, second and third spot was the hardest challenge as there were a great deal of good riders with good scooters.

These events, at this time, were called 'High Speed Trials' for insurance reasons; but, in fact, it was out and out racing. When I look back now I must have been mad as I rode the scooter to all these events with Jan on the back, raced around the track and then rode back home to Morden, Surrey without a thought of how we would get home if I crashed the scooter or broke the engine. As I have said many times before, if you look after your Lambretta, it will be good to you and not let you down!

Even today, you hear people say Lambretta scooters are unreliable which is a load of rubbish. If repairs are properly carried out, the scooter will not give you any trouble.

Cadwell Park high speed trial 1969

Me on my TV 175 Series III on a very wet track. It was a good thing I had brand new Avon Clings for this race.

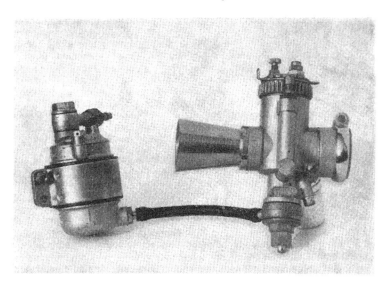

Showing the SS27A Dell'orto carburettor I had on my SX 200. The float was fitted to a thick piece of rubber attached to the frame to help with adjustment and vibration. The carburettor was fitted to a downdraught manifold; no need for a hole in the panel, thank goodness.

It took a bit of setting up, to get the float at the right height and the jetting correct; once that was sorted, it gave a very good performance.

THE FIRST GP 150 IN COUNTRY MY ROAD TEST 1969

The first GP 150 in the UK! Once again, I was adding on the miles before the machine went to the press for road test reports. The run from my home in Morden, Surrey to Headley Heath near Box Hill, Surrey — where I took this photo — proved to be a good test for this scooter.

Most of the journey was uphill, and it was a very good machine to ride with very good performance, about the same as the TV 175 Series III. The machine had good pulling power through the gears, with little vibration. Although the brakes were not bedded-in, they were better than the SX150 model.

One other point: front dampers should have been fitted to this scooter because of the machine's good performance. Still, at the end of the day, it's all comes down to cost.

The ride position was good, although I cannot say I liked the dual seat. I think the Series III type was better. I would have liked a lower saddle, which is probably why the Ancillotti after market seat proved to be very popular on the GP models.

The colour scheme was good and if I had to mark it out of 10 I would give it 9½. So I could not wait for a test ride on the GP 200 model.

Most of the dealers did not like the ink spot, so it was removed. The very first GPs had grey plastic toolboxes, the same as the later SX models, but soon went over to all black plastic. Also, the rear frame and horn grill were aluminium painted black, but were soon changed to black plastic. The bigger 22mm carburettors helped to improve the performance as did the lower frame and leg shields shaved off a little bit of weight which made the scooter handle just that little bit better. This was great if you were into racing at that time. The later GP 200 models had electronic ignition with a new saddle and a modified rear lamp.

GP 200 LAMBRETTA WITH ELECTRONIC IGNITION

Peter Simmonds restored GP 200 Lambretta — Epsom Whirlwinds
Scooter Club.

The road test on the GP 200 was everything I expected, after riding the GP 150 you could feel the extra power from the engine on acceleration. The front dampers made a great difference when breaking hard and helped with the all-round performance of the scooter apart from the saddle. I felt I was sitting up too high. The Ancillotti saddle would have been so much better. This scooter was a winner for all who wanted to race.

SPECIFICATION & PERFORMANCE OF Grand Prix

	FORMULA / 150	FORMULA / 200
PERFORMANCE		
Maximum speed	62.4 m.p.h.; (100,5 Km/h)	68.8 m.p.h. (110,8 Km/h)
Cruising speed	41.5 m.p.h.; (66,8 Km/h)	46.8 m.p.h. (75,4 Km/h)
Acceleration	SS 1/4 mile/21.6 sec	SS 1/4 mile/21.1 sec
	(SS 1 Km/46 sec)	(SS 1 Km/41,3 sec)
Maximum engine output	9.27 b.h.p. (9,4 CV)	11.74 .b.h.p. (11,9 CV)
Fuel consumption	86.2 m.p.g. (30,5 Km/1 l)	70.6 m.p.g. (25 Km/1 l)
(CUNA Specifications)		
ENGINE		
Type	Central, two stroke,	Central, two stroke,
	single cylinder, air cooled	single cylinder, air cooled
Cylinder capacity	9.03 cu. in. (148 cc)	12.08 cu. in. (198 cc)
Bore and stroke	2.24 x 2.28 in. (57 x 58 mm)	2.60 x 2.28 in. (66 x 58 mm)
Compression ratio	8.25 : 1	7.3 : 1
Starting	Kick	Kick
Fuel	Petrol mixture 2⁵/₈	Petrol mixture 4⁵/₈
Gearbox	4 speeds, in constant mesh	4 speeds, in constant mesh
Transmission	Chain drive in oil-bath	Chain drive in oil-bath
Clutch	Multidisc in oil-bath	Multidisc in oil-bath
Tank capacity	1.78 gal. (8,1 l)	1.78 gal. (8,1 l)
FRAME		
Type	Steel tubular chassis	Steel tubular chassis
Wheelbase	50.8 in. (1292 mm)	50.8 in. (1292 mm)
Max length	70.8 in. (1800 mm)	70.8 in. (1800 mm)
Max width	26.8 in. (680 mm)	26.8 in. (680 mm)
Max height	39.8 in. (1012 mm)	39.8 in. (1012 mm)
Seat height	30.39 in. (772 mm)	30.39 in. (772 mm)
Suspension	Front: trailing links	Front: trailing links with helical
	with helical springs	springs and shock absorber
	Rear: swinging crankcase	Rear: swinging crankcase
	and shock absorber unit	and shock absorber unit
Brakes	Drum type	Front: disc type - Rear: drum type
Curb weight	264 lb. (120 kg)	271 lb. (123 kg)
Number of seats	1 + 1	1 + 1
Tyres	Front and rear: 3.50 x 10	Front and rear: 3.50 x 10

LAMBRETTA CONCESSIONAIRES LIMITED Lambretta House, Purley Way, Croydon, Surrey

INNOCENTI

SOC. GENERALE PER L'INDUSTRIA METALLURGICA E MECCANICA

MILANO   ROMA   NEW YORK   PARIGI   LONDRA   CARACAS   DÜSSELDORF

PRINTED IN ITALY 71/69

218

LAMBRETTA AUSTRALIA JOB OFFER

1969 A Job in Australia! No I don't think so!

Lambretta Concessionaires Limited at Croydon, Surrey were taking on the distribution of Lambretta scooters in Australia, along with repairs, spares and accessories. The man that was going out to Australia to run the show spent two or three days with me in the service department to see how everything was done.

He must have liked me as he asked if I would go out with him and run the Service Department; however, it would have been a very big upheaval with two young children, and to leave our families and all our many friends behind — so I said no thanks.

I have often wondered what might have happened if we had gone. We may have been able to find Peter Clarke, who started the Epsom Scooter Club with me. He emigrated to Sydney Australia when I went in the army.

As far as I know, Lambretta (Australasia) Limited were based in 22 Waltham Street, Artarmon, Sydney.

I left Lambretta Concessionaires Limited, Croydon, Surrey in 1970 to work at Roy's of Hornchurch in Essex as Innocenti were soon be stopping production of Lambretta scooters. In hind-sight, this was possibly not the right career move for me!

SOUTHEND RALLY 1969

Here I am competing in the Grass Track Event. Paul Gilbert also used my scooter for these events. He nearly always won, and I was nearly always towards the back of the field.

Every picture tells a tale. This is the morning after the night before. Jan was never a camping person and with two little girls to look after as well — this was probably not the best time to ask where my breakfast was! Jan had cooked 16 breakfasts, before this photograph was taken and could not stomach the thought of eating after that.

RACING AT CADWELL PARK 1969

The photograph shows me on my SX 200 and you can just see the spare petrol tank fitted where the toolbox was. This conversion was used for the Snetterton 12 hour events. I had a new sprayed set of SX 200 panels for everyday use. The cut out in the panel was for an Amal carburettor, fitted by the person who owned the scooter before me. Unfortunately, he had a very bad accident and the scooter was an insurance right-off. I was eventually able to buy the machine from the insurance company. I had the frame straightened, new exchange forks and handlebars, front mudguard, side panels, steering bearings, cables, plus a complete re-spray and engine overhaul. Plus, two new Avon cling tyres and an Ancillotti seat. When racing at this time you had to have large black numbers on a yellow back ground. Paul Gilbert crashed at a grass track meeting before this event and the only handlebars I had at the time were for a GP.

A complete Disc Brake assembly sprayed in white cost £26 18s 0d. If all the parts were brought and made up yourself the cost was £33 0s 0d plus spraying and labour cost to build it up.

Photograph of my carburettor on Page 24 in 'The Lambretta Manual of Performance Tuning and Conversions'. Courtesy of Mrs Edna Calder — Director of Lambretta Concessionaires.

SNETTERTON HIGH SPEED 12 HOUR TRIAL 1969

This event ran from 9 p.m. Saturday until 9 a.m. Sunday and was quite a learning curve for our club. The event required two riders plus a pit crew to carry out the timing of each lap, and to top the scooter up with petrol on each change over. At each change over, the lap, times given at the start were decreased. The next rider had to go faster and faster after each stop.

There was a fantastic array of lights and signals approaching the pits. The hard part was to spot your pit crew as you went by at speed in the dark. I had a 12 volt lighting conversion fitted which was a great help in the pitch black of the Snetterton Circuit. My co-rider was Ray Sweeney for this event, and we got on very well together, and made it into the top ten finishers. I think I am right in saying this was the only time everybody received a certificate for finishing the 12 hour event.

HIGH SPEED TRIAL SNETTERTON 1970

This was my second Snetterton 12 hour speed trial and I made a special screen to keep my hands a little warmer and to protect my stopwatch and lap chart. I had a 12 volt battery conversion with an extra light on right hand side which helped on all the right-hand corners and also to my pit crew when it was dark; they could see me coming long before I got near the line each lap. I also had an extra petrol tank where the toolbox went. In fact, it was a metal toolbox with a plate welded up at the front and all seams welded up all the way around with an LDB cap and tank neck fitted in the front. A petrol tap was fitted at the bottom with a T-connector to the carburettor.

We had been riding for a few hours when the fog came down and I was so thankful for the 3 wheeler headlamp I used, as it had a high and low beam. I could see very well with it, but by now quite a few people had crashed out, so a halt to the race was called. At this time, I was told I was in first place. I was so cold I do not think I took in what they were saying at that moment. I was asked if I would like the event stopped; as I was winning, my answer was 'NO WAY'. If I am going to be a winner, I would like the race to go on if it was safe to do so. A little time after that the fog lifted so we went out again. I had got almost to the end of my time on the track when the fog came down once again and this time the race was stopped, much to the delight of my co-rider Dave Cox. We did land up as the winner which was fantastic.

I packed up our kit and Jan and I rode off home. I have never been as cold as that again, thank goodness. That was a round trip from Morden, Surrey to Snetterton, raced round the track most of the night then rode home again. That's not possible — Lambrettas are not reliable, according to some people.

SNETTERTON

Me racing at Snetterton with the special windscreen and extra 12 volt
light.

HIGH SPEED TRIAL SNETTERTON 1971

This was my third Snetterton event, same old weather; cold and damp. This event was a Le Mans type start, where you had to run across the track, to start your scooter and race off into the darkness.

The scooters were lined up; 225cc went first, then the 200cc and so on 150cc and 125cc. My co-rider was Paul Gilbert. I took the first stint and got a good start. By the time I was half way around the track, I was out in front; my pit crew and I could not believe it (it paid to have very good lights).

I was coming towards the end of my stint, and the cold was really getting into my hands and feet, when the engine went BANG at full speed, just before the bomb hole (if you know Snetterton you will know where I mean.) I don't know what happened, but I was all over the track; thank goodness I did not come off.

I managed to push my scooter back to the pits, but on close inspection the con rod was sticking out of the crankcase. GAME OVER. This was my fault not the scooters as I had checked the other members' scooters who were racing, but not mine as it was going well at the time. I thought it would be ok. This was the only breakdown I ever had in all my years of racing and it came as a great shock to me. One could say a hard lesson learned. No matter how well your scooter is going at the time, always check it out; it will save you money in the end. The only other time I did not finish a race was when I fell off at Lydden Hill.

To all those doubters of Lambretta scooters who thought they were unreliable, I would like to say that Paul Gilbert rode my scooter in the Rough Rides and Grass Track Races, Dave

Cox rode my standard scooter in the Special Class up to 225cc and I rode it in the Standard 200 Class — and also rode it to work every day and out at weekends with the scooter club if I was not racing.

MY TV175 SERIES III

Paul Gilbert displaying his trophies for the British Gas Board Magazine. He was one of the best riders on Rough Rides and Grass Track Racing. The photograph was taken soon after I had my TV 175 re-sprayed in lemon, black and white. Courtesy of Paul Gilbert.

CHAPTER 9
A NEW ERA IN SCOOTERING
THE LAMBRETTA LUNA RANGE

This was a 75cc lightweight, very modern looking scooter. The Vega was the standard model and the Cometa had the lubematic oil injection system.

The little 50cc Luna's were not sold in the UK; but Lambretta Concessionaires at Croydon did have one or two just for assessment. The scooters were too slow for our roads and had no stop light or speedo. I think I am right in saying the headlamp only had a single beam.

The only thing I did not like on these models was the throttle; it was a bit on the heavy side which was a surprise because all the cables were Nylond lined. In the end, we pulled out the inner nylon sleeve to make the throttle lighter.

Courtesy of Mrs Edna Calder — Director
Lambretta Concessionaires Ltd.

LAMBRETTA LUNA RANGE

The Vega was a great little scooter for Grass Track Racing, even more so when they were converted to 125cc and fitted with knobbly tyres. All the engine parts for the conversion came from the Super J Four Speed Scooter. The Vega was not a good seller, fewer than 10,000 were produced. The 50cc model was by far more popular in Italy and almost 30,000 of them were produced. As I said before, they were not sold in the UK and I think I am right in saying they were all white in colour.

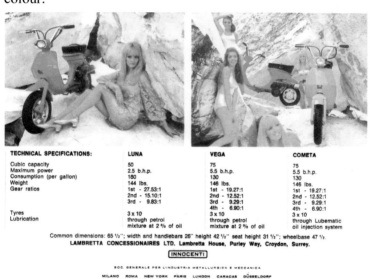

TECHNICAL SPECIFICATIONS:	LUNA	VEGA	COMETA
Cubic capacity	50	75	75
Maximum power	2.5 b.h.p.	5.5 b.h.p.	5.5 b.h.p.
Consumption (per gallon)	180	130	130
Weight	144 lbs.	146 lbs.	146 lbs.
Gear ratios	1st - 27.53:1	1st - 19.27:1	1st - 19.27:1
	2nd - 15.10:1	2nd - 12.52:1	2nd - 12.52:1
	3rd - 9.83:1	3rd - 9.29:1	3rd - 9.29:1
		4th - 6.90:1	4th - 6.90:1
Tyres	3 x 10	3 x 10	3 x 10
Lubrication	through petrol mixture at 2 % of oil	through petrol mixture at 2 % of oil	through Lubematic oil injection system

Common dimensions: 65 ½"; width and handlebars 26" height 42 ½" seat height 31 ½"; wheelbase 47 ½.
LAMBRETTA CONCESSIONAIRES LTD. Lambretta House, Purley Way, Croydon, Surrey.

[INNOCENTI]

SOC. GENERALE PER L'INDUSTRIA METALLURGICA E MECCANICA

MILANO   ROMA   NEW YORK   PARIS   LONDON   CARACAS   DÜSSELDORF

Courtesy of Mrs Edna Calder — Director of Lambretta
Concessionaires Ltd.

Lambretta Concessionaires Limited at Croydon made quite a few accessories for this model. One of these was a front crash bar made out of square section profile and a little upright carrier to take a spare wheel. I understand they were also looking at a little fly screen but, in the end, because of cost they were not produced.

DEALER NET WORK SIGNS — 1956/57

The official number of appointed dealers at this time was round about 200; some were also distributors, like Commerfords Limited, Portsmouth Road, Thames Ditton, Surrey. They were very large motorcycle dealers with premises both sides of the Portsmouth Road. Commerfords Limited had a vast stock of Lambretta scooters and spares and would have quite a number of sub agents who would buy their scooters and spares from them. The company also sold all the accessories, including British made ones as well, which I liked and used to purchase from them when I was working at G & R Garages.

For Lambretta dealers, there were all sorts of signs for the shop front and workshops: some metal, some plastic, some with lights.

Two examples shown below.

Courtesy of Mrs Edna Calder — Director of Lambretta
Concessionaires Ltd.

This is the official Lambretta dealer list from the late fifties.
There were many more dealers not on the list carrying out
service and repairs to Lambretta Scooters.

Courtesy of Mrs Edna Calder — Director of Lambretta Concessionaires Ltd.

Courtesy of Mrs Edna Calder — Director of Lambretta Concessionaires Ltd.

Courtesy of Mrs Edna Calder — Director of Lambretta Concessionaires Ltd.

Courtesy of Mrs Edna Calder — Director of Lambretta Concessionaires Ltd.

LAMBRETTA INNOCENTI MOBILE WORKSHOP VAN

Courtesy of Mrs Edna Calder — Director of Lambretta Concessionaires.

The machine at the far end of the van is to test the magneto for spark, lighting, and battery output. We had the same type of machine in the Lambretta workshop.

There is a pillar drill, hydraulic press and a LI engine in a bracket and loads of cupboard space for parts and tools.

Courtesy of Mrs Edna Calder — Director of Lambretta
Concessionaires. Luton Scooter club members picking up advice from
Innocenti Engineers.

Lambretta

Concessionaires Limited.

TROJAN WORKS · PURLEY WAY · CROYDON · SURREY
Telephone: MUNicipal 2411 (10 lines)   Cables: Lambretta Croydon

FOR IMMEDIATE RELEASE

SIX TONS OF LAMBRETTA
KNOW-HOW!

On the afternoon of Saturday, June 23, six tons of Innocenti
thoroughness in the form of the mobile Service Training Workshop linked
with the dynamic personality of Chief Engineer Sig. Luigi Pini were put
at the disposal of Lambretta clubmen from all parts of Southern England.
This was indeed the opportunity of a lifetime for these keen club
mechanics to obtain expert advice direct from the home of Lambretta.

Derek C. Guy, Secretary of B.L.O.A., welcomed the club representatives
on their arrival and with Dick Beal, Lambretta Technical Service Representative set to solving club members' problems. Though the session was
scheduled to end well before tea time, it was late evening before the
representatives left Trojan Works laden with technical leaflets and with
a great deal of newly acquired knowledge about their favourite topic -
LAMBRETTA.

(Ends)

P.Garnett Keeler   June 29, 1962
Public Relations Officer

Courtesy of Mrs Edna Calder — Director of Lambretta
Concessionaires Ltd. A typical press release from Trojan Works,
Croydon, Surrey.

CHAPTER 10
MY WORKSHOP AND TOOLS

These tools were used for removing the top and bottom frame cones and the one in blue for fitting them back in.

It was always best to remove the top frame cone first so you have a better angle for the tool to remove the bottom cone. Sometimes they were so tight in the frame we had to remove the horn casting and mudguard, so we could knock out the bottom cone. This took three people: one to hold the scooter on an axle stand just forward of the front leg shield struts, and then two people would then hit the bottom cone together until it came out of the frame.

Of course, you would now have to replace the chrome dust cover as it would have quite a bit of damage. If the steering bearings were giving trouble you had to change all six parts together and not just the ball races, as this would not solve the problem.

For the bottom fork cone removal, you needed a long thin punch; there were two holes under the cone for the thin punch to go through to knock out the bottom cone.

SPECIAL STEERING TOOLS SPECIAL TOOLS

Lambretta Concessionaires Limited at Croydon made these special tools to over-come the problem of drilling out broken studs. If the stud had pulled out of the crankcase, you just attached the guide to the crankcase as shown in the picture and drilled out the hole to take the tappex insert. This was made of very hard steel and was also tapered and had a slot cut into it. With the special tool supplied to insert into the crankcase it cuts its own thread. Once completed, you fitted the standard studs back in. The two drill bits had collars on them, to stop you drilling too deep into the crankcase. This is not shown in the picture. It was also possible to fit the insert to the cylinder studs and a special kit was used on the barrel exhaust studs. This complete kit, with inserts, was not cheap for the dealer, but was a must as you could do the job in next to no time, and no broken drill bits or high blood pressure!

The tappex special tools for fitting into the Crankcase.

239

The photo shows a tappex insert with the special tool for fitting into the crankcase and a kit made by Wurth UK Ltd. This also was not cheap, but as I said before it is a must if you want to do a good job and have no more trouble with the silencer studs.

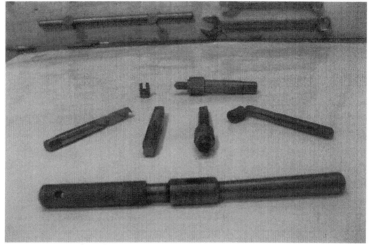

The kit consisted of a drill bit and a tap; a countersink tool and a threaded insert tool. There were no guides with this kit so care had to be taken when drilling out the broken stud as all the work was completed free hand.

The adjustable bar at the bottom of the picture was not part of the kit, but could be brought from any good tool shop.

This picture shows the slot and taper in the tappex insert more clearly. The tapered part with the slot must go in first, so as to cut a good thread. Not as I have seen shown from time to time in the past where people have used a large screw driver in the slots to screw the insert into the case! In this instance, I think the crankcase would have had to be taped out first before screwing in the insert the wrong way round, which would render this job almost useless and give this product a bad name.

Special Tools

This photo shows the re-magnetiser for six pole and four pole flywheels, plus a flux meter to check the flywheels before and after re-magnetising. On the four pole flywheels, you had to work out which was north on the magnets and line it up with the north on the charging head before re-magnetizing. A flux reading of 6 or 7 was very good on the 6 poles and a reading of 8 or over was very good on the four pole flywheels.

This photo shows the rear brake shoe trimmer and it could be used on all models except the TV I75 Series I. If the trouble was a spongy brake it was an advantage to have this tool, more

so if you had pattern brake shoes fitted. Before trimming the brake shoes, you made sure the brake cam was fitted the right way round. There was a little indentation in the cam face; this needed to face upwards so the shoes operated correctly.

These sections of tools in the photo were for all models with a small end bush. The tool would push out the old bush, as you pushed in the new one. It also had a set reamer to finish the job off, so the gudgeon pin would then be a good fit. You could also use an adjustable reamer with a holding bar, shown bottom left of photo.

The next tool shown is for lifting up the scooter to take the rear wheel off. This was made at Lambretta Concessionaires Limited for all models and was much more stable than the one supplied in the scooter tool kit.

On the tool board are some of the tools needed to carry out every day repairs and servicing.

The last tool bottom right is for cutting out the kick start cover for the modified kick start shafts, which had a much thicker shoulder on them. There was also a cutter made for the Cento J range scooters. If you fitted a modified kick start shaft without trimming the case, the shaft would rub on the top plate of the clutch and make the clutch slip.

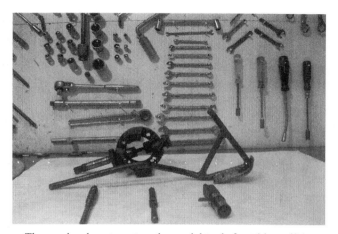

The service department made special tools for taking off the
carburettor on all models, as we were not allowed to knock the
carburettors off the induction manifold with a drift as this action would
damage the carburettor body.

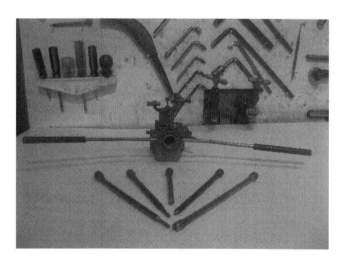

The tools below the carburettor were made by me out of LDB drive
shafts, centre punches, chisels, bearing punch.

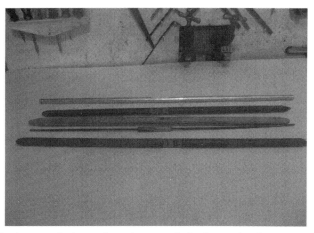

This photograph shows the rods we made in the service department for checking that frames were not bent. A separate rod for each model was made.

We also had a length of steel rope attached to a drill to clean out the exhaust tail pipes on all Series III models not shown in photograph.

The tool in the photo below was made to hold the torque damper unit on the TV 175 Series I, along with a special socket tool to tighten up the damper if it was slipping. You would need a torque wrench, not shown in the picture below, to complete this job.

The torque damper was set between 90—110 ft and in the normal way would not need to be altered. If a side car was fitted the setting went up to 125 ft and that was all you needed to do.

The torque limiter was designed to slip under very aggressive throttle action, or a very hard down change through the gears. This was to protect the drive chain and clutch.

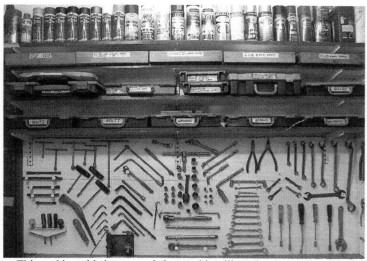

This tool board is in my workshop and is still used today; although, as the years roll by, less and less. A few of the tools I have had since starting out way back in 1956 along with some spare parts books.

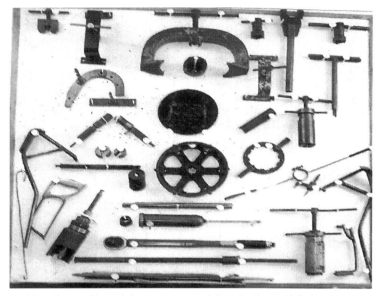

The other tool board shows more special tools. Top middle latest rear hub puller for all models except TVI. In the middle is the brake trimmer for all LI to GP models and bottom of picture is my torque wrench and to the left is the engine mount puller.

The buzz box for checking the timing was dropped after a while because the noise became confusing, if three or four mechanics were all checking the timing at the same time - so we made up a timing light. The battery had to be disconnected from the scooter to carry out this job. In our case, at Lambretta Concessionaires Limited, we had spare batteries to do the job. Once connected up, as on the next page, the bulb would give a bright light as the contacts started to open the light would dim, you had to adjust your contacts or stator plate if the light dimmed before or after your timing mark.

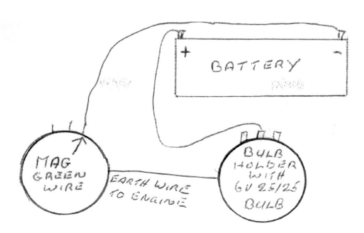

The very latest rear hub puller for all LI and GP hubs.

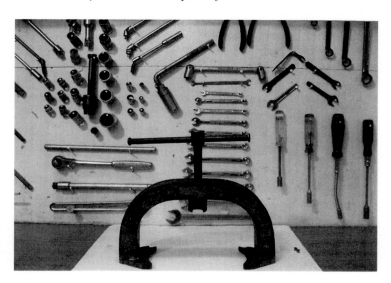

This picture shows the small tank we used to check the petrol consumption on customers scooters. The tank would hold up to a pint of petrol and oil, if you needed to do a long test, or as little as a quarter of a pint for a short test.

The way it was carried out was to run the scooter for a few minutes to get the engine warm, then turn the petrol tap off and let it run on until the petrol in the carburettor runs out, and connect up the test tank. We then had to spin the front wheel until the speedo read a complete mileage i.e. 029290 (which must end with the last digit at zero). The mechanic then rode the scooter at 30 mph until the scooter ran out of petrol and made a note of the mileage.

The hard bit was to work out mpg on the miles completed. We used a stretch strap or tape to keep the tank steady to ensure that all the petrol in the tank was used up.

WORKSHOP AND SERVICE AREA

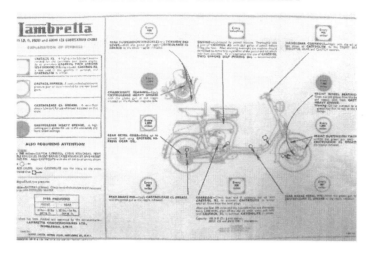

When I first started work on Lambretta machines back in 1956 I had wall charts, as illustrated, for all Lambretta models at the time also for Vespa and Bella scooters. The tool board shows all the tools needed to work on LDB's and TV 175 Series I.

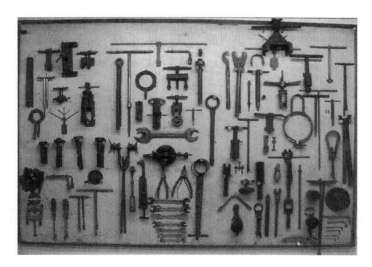

The Bella Scooter was quite a good looking machine, but a bit on the heavy side. I, myself, did not like the heel operated rear brake but having said that, the brakes were good. Servicing was straight forward as long as the chain was kept lubricated and adjusted. As I said before, they did suffer with ignition problems.

I only worked on Bella scooters for a short while, so I am unable to say what other troubles the machine suffered with.

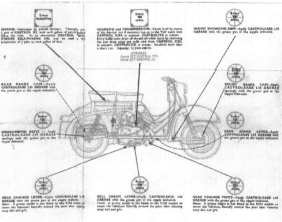

LI SERIES I ENGINE WALL CHART

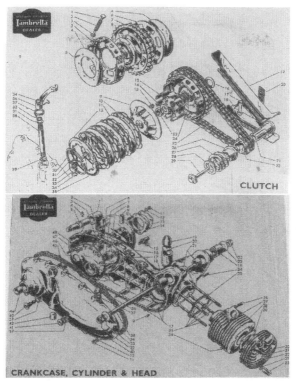

This wall chart shows one of four parts of the LI 150 Series I wall charts of all the engines working parts. A must for the workshop walls way back in 1958. The top part of the picture shows the exploded view of the LI torque damper, which is completely different from TVI torque damper. After a while, when ridden aggressively, the springs would distort or brake, but they were easy to repair. Vespa's also suffered with this problem, but in their case it meant a major engine strip down.

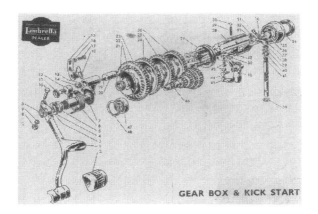

GEAR BOX & KICK START

This wall chart shows the kick start and gearbox layout. The kick start shaft is the part that could fail, and was made much stronger. Shown in red at number 7.

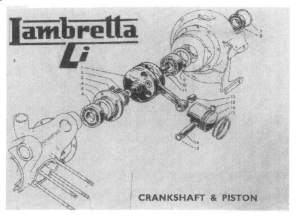

CRANKSHAFT & PISTON

Exploded view of the LI Series I engine parts listed could only be used on this model, main crankcase, crankshaft, barrel/piston, cylinder studs, magneto flange along with the bearing and oil seal. This model had a small end bush not a roller bearing, and a Marelli magneto.

CHAPTER 11
Not All Good Times!
GOING TO COURT FOR LAMBRETTA CONCESSIONAIRES.

This came about when a customer had a Lambretino moped booked in at Lambretta Concessionaires Limited, Croydon for a service. I remembered that he had just had a new tyre fitted by a dealer that was not a standard moped tyre, more like a motorcycle tyre: same rim size, but a deeper tyre bigger in outside diameter. We did not replace the tyre, although it would have been normal standard practice to replace all non-standard parts, but we did inform the customer, suggesting that on his return to Wales he should contact the dealer that had sold the tyre for a correct size replacement; unfortunately, he failed to do so!

The reason we were concerned was that the front number plate was fixed to the top of the front mudguard; the tyre was running too close to the nut and bolt fixing on the number plate.

It was often felt harsh when we removed pattern spares from customer's machines and made them pay for genuine parts. But when you see what Lambretta Concessionaires Limited had to go through at the courts with the Lambrettino moped, just because we had not insisted on changing the front tyre at the service — even though it was brand new — you could understand why. The person who sold the wrong tyre got away scot free.

It was about 6 or 8 months after the service I was called up to the office with regard to the Lambretino and told that Lambretta Concessionaires Limited were being taken to Court. So I went to Wales with Rex White to represent Lambretta Concessionaires Limited and answer any technical questions.

The reason the customer took Lambretta Concessionaires Limited to court was that every time he got to the factory gates of his workplace, the moped seized up and he fell off right in front of his work mates. Obviously, he was embarrassed and lucky for Lambretta Concessionaires Limited he absolutely insisted it kept seizing up on him and that was the cause of him falling off.

I explained that, in fact, it was impossible for this to happen, due to the machine being an automatic. As soon as the engine stopped, there would be no drive to the rear wheel so this was not the cause of him falling off. In his statement, he said it was difficult getting into the factory gates because of the high camber on the road and a high slope up to the gates. We offered to take the cylinder head off to show it had not seized up.

The customer lost the case against Lambretta Concessionaires Limited, which was very lucky as it was that oversized tyre that had been the problem. It had caught the bolts holding the front number plate when he hit the deep gully by the factory entrance which pushed the front suspension right down. This locked up the front wheel and threw him off his moped.

It had been a very stressful day and Rex and I were relieved making our way back home. What you might call our longest day! Rex had picked me up about 4am from my house in Morden, Surrey and drove all the way to Swansea in Wales. We had spent all day in Court and then drove all the way back and arrived home around midnight. We stopped at the Severn Bridge on the way down for breakfast and stopped there on our way back for a rest and meal. It was hard going for Rex and me at work the next day.

THE ACCIDENTS AND BRUSH WITH THE LAW!

Returning home from a club run from Newhaven, two of our members were knocked off their scooter: Margaret and Mike Smallbone. The motorist had tried to overtake all of our club members on a bend in the road with double white lines, when a car came around the bend towards us. The car overtaking us had to cut in and knocked Mike and Margaret off their scooter. Margaret came off worse with a very bad ankle which took months to heal, along with a badly damaged hand and engagement ring. Mike suffered a few cuts and a bruised shoulder, but would not go to hospital. They both had a painful journey home and went to the doctors the next day. Mike was told he had dislocated his shoulder. They were both off work for a few weeks.

Just to make matters worse, another car driver run into the back of their scooter sometime later. I was working at G & R Garage Limited, when I picked up their damaged scooter and took it to work for repair. We now had to sort out two insurance claims.

It was sometime later we went to Court at Lewis, Sussex. I had to go as I was a witness to the first accident. We only won the case in the end because the person driving the car towards us was an ex-policeman, which was just as well as Mike's solicitor failed to turn up at court. He had too many cases to deal with, so just wrote a letter to the judge with regard to the case.

DEVON HOLIDAY WITH OUR SCOOTER CLUB

Mike and Margaret had a third accident going on holiday to Ilfracombe, North Devon with our scooter club; he touched the side of a bridge with his tent poles on the back of the scooter. So off to hospital for a check-up but thank goodness both were OK. The rest of the Bank Holiday break was brilliant.

On packing up to come home, the heavens opened and did not stop all day. We had been riding for about three hours and were about as wet as one can get. I was out in front and just entering a small town when a policeman stepped out from a shop doorway and put his hand up to stop us. I skidded to a halt. "I cannot see your number plate," I was greeted with. "You are nicked!" I had a front carrier with my tent and a small bag on it. My front number plates were on each side of the front mudguard. There was no way he could not see them. Just like all of us he was cold and wet, and the next vehicle that came around the corner was going to get nicked, just my luck it was me! Sometime later, I received a letter from the Chief Constable informing me that if I was caught in their area again I will be severely dealt with. My respect for the police after that took a nosedive.

Unfortunately, this was not my first brush with the police. I was driving the work's Ford van along the Kingston bypass going to Lambretta Concessionaires Limited at Wimbledon for spares, when I heard a ringing in my ears and a car overtook me on the inside, and then cut in front of me and shuddered to a halt with me skidding into the fast lane. Out jumped two policemen: one to direct the traffic round us, the other to give me a good telling off. I had been speeding at over 40 mph. In those days a van had to stick to 30/40 mph. I am not sure how much of a fine I received and my driving licence was endorsed. My boss was not impressed; once again, a hard lesson learned.

TIME TO MOVE ON

I had been approached by Roy Cary several times on his visits to Lambretta Concessionaires Limited with an offer to manage his shop in Hornchurch, Essex. Some of our club members had been to Roy's of Hornchurch and thought the shop was a gold mine of spares and accessories.

After much discussion with my wife Janet, we decided that we would move to Hornchurch. It was a very big wrench to move away from our families, lovely home, Jean and Jim Galea — the best neighbours anybody could wish for — and our many friends, with two very small children. It was going to be very stressful.

Before I moved on from Lambretta Concessionaires Limited, I would just like to say that of all the scooters produced around the world, in my opinion, Lambretta machines came out top. Not one other make of scooter had a better handlebar layout which started back in 1952 with the early LD when all the handlebar control cables were covered in plastic sleeving.

Onto the LI and TV's with totally enclosed handlebars which were very stylish and easy to work on when doing repairs, plus very clean stylish body lines as the advert stated,

"There are none better than Lambretta." They were second to none with their after sales service and spare parts back up.

So now the time has come to say goodbye to everybody I have worked with over the past 6 or 7 years. It was much harder than I thought, more so when I was presented with a good luck card signed by most of the people working there and a gift for our new home in Hornchurch, Essex.

Royspeed at the 70th anniversary of Innocenti, a very sad time for me to see the factory as it is now.

Dick with the Royspeed banner outside what is left of the Innocenti Factory.

MY LEAVING CARD FROM LAMBRETTA
CONCESSIONAIRES LIMITED WITH SO MANY NAMES
OF FRIENDS AND WORK MATES

Mr PJ Agg and Mrs Calder also signed my leaving card.

Greetings
and all good wishes
Good luck
P. Hogan
Mrs. T.
we shall miss you
all the very best
Julie
Best Wishes
Best Wishes
Vicky
GOOD LUCK
Thanks for all your help
Best Wishes
Audrey

CHAPTER 12
MOVING ONCE AGAIN
OUR NEW HOME IN HORNCHURCH, ESSEX

We were gazumped right at the last minute on our new home in Hornchurch, Essex. We had sold our maisonette in Morden, Surrey on the first day of it being on the market. A very nice young couple fell in love with the property and decided they wanted it. Our wonderful neighbours, who shared a veranda at the rear of the building with us, got on fairly well with the new owners.

As I started my new job in February 1970, I had nowhere to live. My new boss Roy and his wife Brenda offered me a roof over my head for a couple of weeks until I found a flat for myself and family. I had expected to be settled into our new home by then.

A few days later, after having looked everywhere for us to live, I found a new housing estate being built on the old Hornchurch Airfield. Jan and I decided to take one after Jan's father made sure they were built professionally. The house would be ready in a few weeks. In the end, a few weeks turned into five months. In the meantime, we had to live somewhere. We ended up in a flat above a car showroom at Upminster Bridge, Essex beside the tube and rail station.

We moved into our new home on 3rd August, 1970.

This is the garden of our newly built house.

A NEW START AT ROY'S OF HORNCHURCH SCOOTER SHOP.

My first week at Roy's of Hornchurch was, to say at the very least, an eye opener. Gone was the ordered work routine and knowing everybody around you. I had both workshop and shop staff to manage. Terry Shea, Roy's out-going manager, was still there working out his notice to the end of the month, which was stressful enough without the confusion it caused to all the staff.

One good thing Terry did for Jan and I was to find the flat at Upminster Bridge. It was in a poor state, but it would only be for a short while; if only that had been true. We all know what builders are like, as already mentioned, a few weeks turned into five months.

When Jan and the girls arrived at Upminster Bridge flat, just before Easter, the removal van arrived and the men took one look at the flat and said "You cannot stay here, let us take you back?" It was only when Jan said we have a new house being built they relented and took most of our belongings into storage. It goes without saying what the place was like. Jan soon got the flat liveable. During the next few months, the flat was more often than not filled with Epsom Whirlwind members and friends; no change from Tudor Drive then!

Roy's shop was an absolute gold mine of accessories. The vast stocks of spares were all over the place. It took some time to sort out and price up, so staff did not have to look up the price in the spares book.

All Club members were given 10% discount on any purchases including, at the time, Bardahl oils; plus a free coffee for everybody that came into the shop.

It was about this time the late Doug May came to work at the shop. The late Frank Harris ran the workshop with a couple of lads called Peter and Tony.

The shop had a Royspeed GP 125 Lambretta which was raced by Tom Pead, a member of the local scooter club 'The Companions'. The club had a very large amount of members and they almost lived in the shop all the time. Another long-term member of the club was John Roberts, who still has some scooters today. He bought his first car from me to learn to drive.

I still raced at this time and a very young Doug May took to the racing scene. He only had an old LI 150 Series II Lambretta at the time, but soon changed to a much better scooter. His last scooter was a GP 200.

We also had a lad called Paul who came to work for Roy; he stayed for about three years.

A man called Colin became a very good friend of mine, and was the owner of Colwood Motors before he retired. They carried out a lot of our service and repairs plus MOTs on our vehicles. His premises were about 300 yards from Roy's shop. I still go there today for my car servicing and MOTs. Paul, who used to work for Roy way back then, now runs the MOT side for Colin at Colwood Motors, and of course scooters come into the conversation at some point in time.

The photo shows the inside of Roy's shop. Not an inch of room left to put up more accessories. As you can see, we also sold and serviced Vespa scooters.

ROYSPEED BOLT-ON POWER

The illustrations below are part of the booklet given out to customers showing just some of the products the shop sold.

BOLT ON POWER !!!

AND ACCELERATE
INTO THE 70's
WITH

Royspeed

ENGINE

CONVERSIONS

FROM

ROY of Hornchurch
35 HIGH STREET, HORNCHURCH, ESSEX
TELEPHONE: HORNCHURCH 42323

Dear Scooter owner,

I would like to introduce you to our latest range of Royspeed Conversions and Accessories which you will no doubt appreciate are very reasonably priced and of consistent high quality. As we specialise only in Lambrettas and Vespas and are Main Agents for both makes you can rest assured that the special parts we offer to you have come onto the market only after extensive research by our workshop into the efficiency and reliablity of all our specialist equipment. Only after years of experience in these two makes are we now prepared to offer the advanced equipment that experience has evolved. For too long now scooter modifications such as ours have always been something like a dark and unknown mystery and the subject of modifying and tuning to a higher level of efficiency for the average owner, has always been a matter of much trial and many an expensive error, without a very satisfactory result. Now with our comprehensive range of 'Royspeed' 'Bolt-on Power' Conversions all that is over. We hope in the future that you, like so many other Scooterists, will have the opportunity of enjoying the new cheap, easy and reliable way of increasing the comfort, efficiency and power output of your scooter.

Roy

OUR WORLD, LIKE YOURS, IS CENTRED AROUND SCOOTERS. WE PUT OUR HEART AND SOUL INTO MAKING OUR BUSINESS A SUCCESSFUL ONE. BUT AT THE SAME TIME WE ARE DEEPLY CONCERNED WITH THE WAY PRICES ARE RISING AND WHAT THIS MEANS TO THE AVERAGE SCOOTER OWNER. WE HOPE WE CAN BE OF SERVICE TO YOU WITH THE GOODS YOU WANT AT THE PRICES YOU CAN AFFORD.

Courtesy of Roy's of Hornchurch.

REMEMBER THAT WE GIVE

10% DISCOUNT

TO ALL SCOOTER CLUB MEMBERS

Please note we are Main Agents for **LAMBRETTA** and **VESPA** and can supply all Spares and Accessories by return of post. We **CHALLENGE** you to try us for anything you find unobtainable.

TRADE ENQUIRIES WELCOMED

Please remember to enclose two shillings in the pound to cover postage and packing. All orders should be sent to Dept

Due to our Policy of continuous improvement and development we reserve the right to alter Prices and Specifications at any time.

Page 6   *NOV 1970*   COPY FOR RETURN
OF ALTERATIONS

ROY of Hornchurch (Enterprises) Ltd.
ROYSPEED CONVERSIONS
35 HIGH STREET,
HORNCHURCH,
ESSEX.   Bolt on Power
Telephone: Hornchurch 42323   Accessories

WE STILL SAY WE OFFER MORE FOR
"THE CLUB SCOOTERIST" - THAN THE OTHERS
WE STARTED THE 10% DISCOUNT AND WE STILL
GIVE IT - EVEN AT OUR PRICES !!!!

WE ARE THE 30mm DEL ORTO PEOPLE --
WE STOCK THE SPARES
350 X 10 AVON CLING TYRES   45/-
400 X 10 AVON CLING TYRES   59/6
SERENE REAR CARRIERS BLACK PLASTIC COVERED   38/-
72 mm PISTON S   50/-
60 mm PISTONS   38/-
500 & 67mm BORGO PISTONS   50/-
8X 200 STANDARD SILENCERS   65/-
COMPETITION CLUTCH PLATES & SPRINGS   30/-
BALL END LEVERS   pair   18/-
DOUBLE ENGINE MOUNTS & BAR   79/6
BRAKE SHOES   37/6
BELL MOUTHS WITH FILTER FOR AMALS   15/-
METAL AIR FILTER FOR VEGAS & AMALS   17/6
LEVER COVERS   pair   4/-
GRAND-PRIX FIBRE-GLASS SIDE PANEL SET each 90/-
NOW YOU KNOW WHY THERE IS A --
"GOLDSTRIKE AT ROYS"
REMEMBER 20% DISCOUNT ON BARDAHL
NEW MACHINES THE BEST VALUE
MONEY CAN BUY
WE BOAST THE FASTEST RETURN OF POST
SERVICE IN THE TRADE
Remember theres a cup of coffee or coke when
you arrive
YOU WON'T BE DISAPPOINTED
Roy of Hornchurch -- 35 High Street, Hornchurch
Essex

265

SANDOWN, ISLE OF WIGHT EASTER WEEKEND RALLY 1970

My first big event since starting at Roy's of Hornchurch. I went on my scooter and Jan came by train with our girls Stephanie and Debbie, which was a trial in its self. Least said the better!

Our club 'Epsom Whirlwinds', stayed in chalets on the cliff top at Sandown and we all had a cracking weekend and enjoyed all events.

Saturday started with a road trial which about 100 people entered. Unfortunately, all I can remember, it was very wet and cold.

Even though the course for the sand racing had to be moved, due to the tide, it was the 'highlight' of the weekend. On Sunday, Doug May and I entered the sand race. But we both got tangled up with each other at the start. His rear footboard went over my kick-start pedal somehow and, by the time we pulled apart we were right at the back of the field. So that was that.

The most difficult part of the day was getting down onto the beach, and back up again, when the racing was over. The event finished in time for the Easter Parade. Roy's pick up van bedecked in "undies" and a training potty was a great sight.

Monday was wet and windy for the hill climb event, and many braved the storm. Ron Moss, Doug and I entered along with many others and were glad when it was all over, as we were all very wet and cold and it was almost time to return home.

I took Jan and the children back to the station in the van then dashed back to pack the rest of the kit away and head for the ferry with some of the boys from Hornchurch. The ride home was uneventful, thank goodness.

BURNING RUBBER AT FULBECK SPRINT 1970

1970 was the start of the fulbeck sprints for me. I was to test out a 30mm Delorto Carburettor, which Roy had brought back from Italy. I had adapted it to an Amal Manifold because the down draft manifolds were not available at that time, plus only a few jets to play with. It worked well, so it was the start of Roy's of Hornchurch selling 30mm Delorto Carburettors, along with hundreds of Jets and spares through the shop and to the trade. Good old Fred Willingham showed us all the way to sprint a Lambretta.

by NICK BARNES

Dave Cox and myself started off Sunday morning for R.A.F. Fulbeck with two bikes and gear loaded into the back of a Lambretta three wheeler. It took us about 2½ hours to get there, not a fast time, but at least it was dry and fairly warm, and we arrived about ½ hour before the start. Having unloaded the bikes, Dave had his 150 scrutineered but I was having trouble with the jetting in the carb., but I managed to rectify this in time for the start. Already there was a lot more people there than I expected. I noticed Fred Willingham with his very quick Special and names like Chris Watson, Dick Sedgeley and John Ronald were in attendance.

Dave and I had decided to use each other's bikes to make things more interesting but this was later to prove even more so with our number set up. The day had started off sunny but of course the rain had to come in short showers, but this did not slow things up at all, in fact the organisation was very good. When we stopped for lunch everybody had completed two runs and things were getting very interesting. Fred had put up two 15 second times. The rain continued into the afternoon and some more good times were set up making our close rivals to be Dick and John on 125s and Chris on his 150. At the end of the day everybody had completed 5 runs and a good time was had by all.

Peterborough Sprint *WINNERS*

Class A & B: Nick Barnes. Class C: Nick Barnes. Class D: Dick Sedgeley. Class E: M. Collins. Team Award: Lambretta Club London. Best Lady: Carole Carter. Fastest Time of Day: Fred Willingham.

Courtesy of Nick Barnes.

COMAKS 70

FIELD EVENT OF THE YEAR

by Chuck Swannell

COMAKS 70 was a new idea for a Rally. It was promoted by the Companions Scooter Club and the Rakes Lambretta Club. The title was taken from a combination of both Club names.

The site chosen by the Committee — Bedfords Park, Havering-atte-Bower, nr. Romford, was first class as a rally venue. Plenty of open space, to have a varied programme of events.

Saturday afternoon, the main feature was the Sprint, along a tree-lined lane with a few curves and a chicane. Despite a loose shale surface, some very good times were achieved. After the Sprint came the Bar-b-q, held in the open air around the restaurant. The evening was dry and warm which lent itself the Disco style music and the awards for the Sprint were presented during the evening, which finished with a sing-song on the camp site.

Sunday morning produced more field events, including a hill climb, with the star attraction of the Grass Track Racing. An extremely good course making full use of the natural surroundings made the racing very exciting.

So to finish — a short report on Comaks 70 — a very good rally that deserved an even greater attendance — which it will doubtless get if it is put on again next year. Thank you for a very enjoyable weekend.

RESULTS

Sprint - Class 'A'		*Class 'B'*	
1. J. Ronald	- Nottingham	1. P. Gilbert	- Epsom
2. A. Smith	- Kensington	2. B. Hull	- Bromley
3. N. Orr	- Kensington	3. D. Wilfang	- Vikings

Hill Climb - Class 'A'		*Class 'B'*	
1. N. Frost	- Bromley	1. T. Muddimer	- Leicester
2. J. Ronald	- Nottingham	2. B. Hull	- Bromley
3. A. Smith	- Bromley	3. P. Hockley	- Hamps. Union

Grass Track Racing - Class 'A'		*Class 'B'*	
1. N. Frost	- Bromley	1. P. Hockley	- Hamps. Union
2. K. Brickclbank	- Luton	2. K. Reilly	- Kensington
3. C. Gooding	- Broadsmen	3. D. Hall	- Bedford

Class 'C'		*Class 'D'*	
1. P. Gilbert	- Epsom	1. P. Meads	- Luton
2. J. Taylor	- Luton	2. D. Pinkney	-
3. B. Hull	- Bromley	3. J. Newman	- Thorne

Rally Champ.	*Lady Champ*
B. Hull	Bev Flanagan

5

Courtesy of John Roberts.

Paul Gilbert on my SX 200 in front of the late John Taylor on his Special Lambretta. John was a really good bloke and a top rider in this type of event. Courtesy of Chuck Swonnell.

ROYS OF HORNCHURCH

One of the things I changed in the shop was to push the sales of Filtrate Oils and Cromwell Crash Helmets. I still have my first full face Cromwell Helmet today, 'just as a keep sake'. Cromwell was the first manufacturer to make a full face crash helmet for motorcycles. They also made helmets for the R.A.F. pilots, and other special projects. The motorcycle helmet was made of fibre glass, with all leather trim inside and very thick visors that could withstand a shot gun blast.

Another product Roy brought in from Italy was the Ducati Electronic Ignition Kits for the G.P.S. It was about this time that Ron Moss closed his 'Supertune' shop in Croydon and came to work for Roy. Ron had his own big bore silencer, but it was too expensive to make for sale.

The work load for scooter tuning was getting out of hand

268

so it was decided our tuned barrels and piston should be made in Italy for 125cc/150cc/200cc. We could also supply barrels for 175cc and 225cc scooters; all with high compression heads. I also made my own big bore silencer, which had taken a lot of time and welding.

Roy was selling the Ancillotti big bore, but we decided to make our own big bore from a standard silencer. The 40mm U tube was made by a tube bending firm in Harlow, Essex. The solid copper gasket and plate, plus the big bore flange and welding were carried out by Mr. Coker, an engineer in Southend. Lambretta Concessionaires Limited would only supply us with a hundred silencers at a time so as not to run short of stock for other dealers. This put a strain on us price wise as we were making all these products to sell to the trade as well as our customers.

When Mr Coker became ill and was unable to work, we had to look for another engineering firm to carry out the work. This was also our chance to make a bigger U tube 44mm diameter. This time the draw back was that the firm was based in Southampton, and meant the best part of the day on the round trip; putting more cost to the end product.

We also had a re-boring machine, so we could re-bore a customer's barrel while they waited. In some cases the customer rode to the shop took the barrel off themselves waited for it to be re-bored, and re-fitted it again.

We also had a bubble packing machine to enhance our smaller trade products, such as competition clutch plates, clutch springs, solid copper exhaust gaskets, and brake shoes for LI and GP models, plus sprint stickers in six colours. This all saved time when packing up orders that came by post or phone each day and they were sent out in the afternoon post.

Courtesy of Roy's of Hornchurch.

MYSTERY OF THE LOFT AT ROY'S OF HORNCHURCH

There have been many stories told about what was stored in the loft. When I started working at Roy's in 1970, all LDB parts, some LI and TV Series I parts and some old windscreens, were stored there. The remainder of the space was taken up by Avon Cling Tyres which we used to buy; about 500 at a time. This proved to be a bit too much weight in the loft and we had to do a very quick shoring-up of both floors to prevent a disaster falling on our heads.

We were all in the shop at the time when there was a sharp crack and a lot of dust. Ron Moss was very quick on the race track, but on this occasion he was much quicker! He was out the shop like a rocket, and back in again because he left his wallet or fags behind and he still beat the rest of us to the door! After that experience, less was stored in the loft.

There was one room upstairs for the office, and the other three rooms were full up with spares and accessories, crash helmets and clothing.

We had more storage space out the back of the shop, where we had two tea chests full up with rear damper springs; one for the small springs and one for the large springs. Two chests full up with fork links, one left and one right and another one was full up with LDB HT coils and other electrical parts.

Further back still was the workshop with enough room for four people to work, plus an area for spraying.

We also did MOTs while you waited.

CRYSTAL PALACE RACE — SEPTEMBER 1970

Roy attended this event. Ron was going like a rocket when he overheard two lads talking about Ron's scooter, he had five gears, and thought that was why he was going so quickly. This was not true at that time, but started Roy thinking about a five speed gearbox. Even after I had explained to him Lambretta

Concessionaires Limited at Croydon had looked into having a five speed conversion and dropped the idea because of cost.

Roy was not put off and went the lower cost way with thinner gears, and gear group plus selector and spring, all to fit on the standard LI or GP lay shaft.

The handlebar gear control had to be re-stamped with five gear numbers. The first batch received were OK, but the second batch, for some reason, were made wrong and gave us a lot of problems so further orders from Italy were cancelled.

The first batch of five speed boxes arrived towards the end of May 1971.

1971 — ALL THE NEW SCOOTERS FOR SALE
OUTSIDE THE FRONT OF ROY'S SHOP.

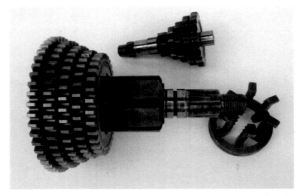

Here we have all five gears fitted to the lay shaft, along with the gear group and gear selector.

FIVE SPEED GEAR BOX BY ROYSPEED

The Five Speed in a cut away gear casing on the counter at the London Motorcycle Show along with all our other products.

Typical Roy's of Hornchurch stand at the London Motorcycle show. Showing all Royspeed products.

LONDON MOTORCYCLE SHOW JANUARY 1972

Our stand at the London Motorcycle Show. The large mini-flake spray can and base was made by the late Mike Karslake. On the board at the back of the stand are our big bore silencers, sprayed in our wrinkle finish paint. We also made a big bore U tube and flange kit that could be welded to the customers own silencer.

All the products in the picture were sold to the trade as well as retail customers. The bubble packed clutch plates, springs and the solid copper exhaust gaskets are on the wall above the large mini flake display. The side panels and front mudguard on display were made of fibre glass; these were fitted to all our Special Royspeed Tuned Scooters.

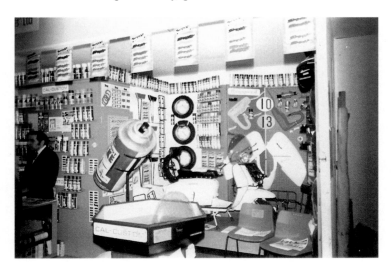

LCGB AGM 1972

I was presented with these two framed photographs by LCGB at their AGM in 1972, in recognition of the spares support we gave to all Lambretta members taking part in competition events. I believe the two photographs were taken at the Leicester Grass Track Meeting. The other person, far left, in the photograph is John Roberts of the Companions Scooter Club. He is still into Scootering today, and we are still in touch with each other. Unfortunately, I cannot remember the other person's name in the photograph. I am still in contact with one other member from the Companions Scooter Club, Pete Maisey, who calls round from time to time to see me on his trusty Lambretta.

ROY'S OF HORNCHURCH SERVICE VAN

These are the photographs presented to me at the grass track meeting we attended.

THRUXTON RACE CIRCUIT.

Thruxton was about four miles past Andover on the A303. It was a very fast open and flat circuit as it was part of an old airfield. The meeting was organized by L.A.S.C.A. I took my scooter in the Royspeed van with lots of spares, which Jan looked after for me while I was on the track, which was in two parts. I came third in both races behind Ron Moss and Ray Kemp. This was my last race on the track as the demand for spares at the meeting was so high, so from now on I would concentrate on just selling the spares from the van.

My third place trophy.

ISLE OF MAN

We attended the Isle of Man rally two years running with the spares van, but before we could go, we had to obtain a peddlers licence from the I.O.M. authority. We also needed a letter from the local scooter dealer in Douglas to say we were not taking away his trade. As luck would have it, we were selling Royspeed parts to him already and would be taking quite a lot of spares with us for him to sell. On arrival at Douglas, I had to call at the police station with all my paperwork to make sure, I was of good character and everything was in order.

The week went very well and a large amount of the £6,000 stock on the van was sold. Even so it would not be enough to offset the cost of going to the I.O.M. for a week. One good thing that came out of this was that I met Jack, a Lambretta dealer, from Rhyl in North Wales. He was very impressed with our Royspeed products and how well they sold. We would be trading parts with Jack for quite a few years. We became friends and he stayed at our house when he came to Hornchurch from time to time until he became very ill and sadly passed away. He is still remembered when we talk about days gone by.

The "22" Lambretta Club

Championship is Sponsored by
✻   ✻   ✻
LAMBRETTA CONCESSIONAIRES LTD
✻   ✻   ✻
ROY of HORNCHURCH
✻   ✻   ✻
CROSS KEYS - PULLOX HILL
✻   ✻   ✻
DUCKHAMS

PLEASE SUPPORT YOUR
SPONSORS FOR 1972

JET SET EDITOR

Mr. RALPH HYDE

16 Western Gardens
Western Boulevard
Nottingham NG8 2GP

Lambretta club
GREAT BRITAIN

Calendar of
Championship
Events 1972

278

March		Points
19th	Leicester Sporting Trial	....
April		
1st-3rd	Isle of Wight Rally	....
16th	Sprint (R.A.F. Fulbeck)	....
23rd	Yeovil GT	....
30th	Northern Hill Climb	....
May		
6th-7th	Tour of Wales	....
21st	Cadwell Park	....
27th-28th	Comaks 1972 Rally GT	....
June		
4th	Lincoln GT	....
17th-24th	Isle of Man GT	....
July		
1st-2nd	Starlight Trial	....
9th	Bristol GT	....
August		
13th	Sprint (R.A.F. Fulbeck)	....
26th-28th	Southend International Western Rodeo Rally GT	....
September		
9th-10th	Western 250	....
17th	Norwich GT	....
23rd-24th	Manchester Rally GT	....
October		
8th	Edge Hill Sporting Trial	....
15th	Sprint (Curbrough)	....
November		
11th	Annual General Meeting	

FOR YOUR INFORMATION

L.C.G.B. General Secretary
Mr. J. Ronald
10 Steeles Way, Lambley, Nottingham

Administration Secretary, Championship Points
Membership
Mr. G. R. Gostelow
33 Moore Road, Mapperley, Nottm. NG3 6EF

P.R.O.
Regulations for all L.C.G.B. Promoted Events
Mr. R. Cheetham
7 North Street, Langley Mill, Nottm. NG16 4BS

Treasurer
Mr. M. M. Caporn
11 Newholm Drive, Wilford, Nottingham

Federation Competition Licences
Mr. A. Mills
19 Nook Farm Avenue, Syke, Rochdale, Lancs.

Courtesy of Lambretta Club Great Britain.

The expense of running the van for scooter events was getting out of hand; so it was with great regret that we had to call a halt to this service. The very high insurance cost on the van, plus all the managers at the race circuits wanting a fee, plus 10% discount on parts we gave everybody, was not cost effective. If I had been paid for doing this extra work, the losses would have been even greater!

It was also time for me to pack up racing and spend more time with my family. Our club had a good day with Bill Brunning coming 3rd in his class and myself coming 2nd in mine.

This was my last sprint meeting at R.A.F. Fulbeck with my two daughters sitting in the back of my car.

LONDON MOTORCYCLE SHOW

Once again we are back at the London Motorcycle Show selling mainly Filtrate oils, Cromwell Helmets, Cal Custom Spray paints and Sprex very high temperature paints. Our Filtrate rep at this time was Tom Knapper. We were selling a great deal of Filtrate oil, and he persuaded us to take on the distribution of all Filtrate products to the trade for Essex, Kent and London.

This photograph shows how I looked after a 12 hour stint on a show stand.

ROY'S OF HORNCHURCH — ELDERLY SHOPPERS

We had several older customers at Roy's of Hornchurch shop. One gentleman brought a new Vespa 90 in exchange for his old Lambretta, because it was much lighter to handle. The gentleman at least eighty years old at the time.

We sold a GP 150 to another older customer and we re-purchased the machine about three years later with only 300 miles on the clock. It had not had its first service check done.

Another long term customer had a LI 150 Series I Reg. No. 782GKL which we bought back off him because he was unable to ride it anymore. He gave us the book he had kept to record every item he bought, every service he had done and even how much petrol and oil he purchased over all the years he owned the scooter. The tool roll and handbook were in perfect condition and all the inner cable ends had been wound with very fine wire and then soldered to stop them fraying. I sold the scooter to Mike Karslake for his museum.

The photograph shows my two daughters on board at the 1978
Southend rally, which was organised by Mike Karslake. This is the
scooter that was used in the Citizen Smith television series and rode by
Robert Lindsay playing 'Wolfie'.

CHANGE OF MANAGEMENT AT ROY'S OF HORNCHURCH

Roy sold his shop to Terry Shea, around 1980, as he wanted to
expand his Fantic motorcycle and moped business further. So
the shop was renamed Enterprise Motorcycles in line with our
Enterprise products for the trade.

We had a triple stand at the London Motorcycle Show.

The mini spray can was re-painted to look like a Filtrate Linklyfe chain spray. The large can was attached to a Fantic moped frame. A long tube from the spray head to the chain was fitted to make it look as if you were spraying the chain. The wheel was very slowly turned around by a small electric motor. Unfortunately, we were unable to demonstrate this, because of safety; even-so it was a very big seller at the show along with the black Sperex V.H.T. spray paint.

Our day started at 7 a.m. leaving the shop with more stock. It would take us about two hours to get to Westminster Halls; about 20 miles (32.186.9 km) and put the new stock on the stand, park the van for the day and be ready by 10 am when the doors opened to the public for the next 10 hours. Then it was back to the shop to top up with more stock and home for a few hours' sleep.

I asked Filtrate Oils Limited if they would supply me with a folder to keep all their product sheets together for the show and for my trade customers.

When Filtrate Colloidal Graphite (the black stuff) was produced for two stroke motorcycles and scooters the oil came in tins with an oil measure in the screw lid. This was very handy, especially if you were going on a long trip.

Filtrate folder on the right with all the leaflets inside on all products the Trade could purchase.

Some garages had five gallon drums of oil with a tap at the bottom and used an oil measure can. Other garages had a container with a plunger you push down to get the right amount of oil you needed into your tank. They were prone to getting an air lock in the delivery hose to your tank if not kept fairly full up with oil.

There was also a special two stroke petrol pump that delivered, at the turn of a dial, the right petrol/oil ratio to your

scooter. Once again if they were not kept topped up an airlock could occur and not too far down the road your engine would seize up. I always found it better to take your own oil with you.

My thanks go to our new representative, Ron Slade. He was a great help to us, especially when working at the motorcycle shows.

We kept in touch until Ron sadly passed away after a short illness.

SPANISH — ROYSPEED

The shop sold a reasonable amount of Spanish Lambretta scooters. The last of the standard type was a metallic blue model with the LI 150 III front mudguard. The very last Spanish (Servetta) Lambretta the shop sold was a 125 Royspeed, as seen below.

The machine was last seen in Mike Karskake's museum in Devon.

Later Enterprise Motorcycles were selling the GP imported by Two Four Accessories from India. The first machines to arrive were not too bad, as a lot of the parts were from Innocenti and the carburettor was Delorto. After that, things went downhill somewhat. One of the problems was damage to the scooters as they were in wooden crates in the bottom of the ship hold with tea chests on top of them. There were quite a lot of tea stains on the paint work. A good clean and polish took care of some of the stains, but sometimes a bit of re-spraying had to be carried out.

CHAPTER 13
BIG CHANGES AT ROY'S OF HORNCHURCH
Enterprise Motorcycles

I purchased 12 Indian GP 150's in light blue at an auction from the Chelmsford area. I think they were used by the London Borough of Hammersmith as "run-arounds" for their staff. They were in a poor condition and had no rubber stand feet, instead they had metal plates welded to the stand legs. They were re-sprayed in our mini flake colours, overhauled plus MOT. Within a few weeks they were all sold, which gave the shop a boost.

Most of our time was spent selling Vespa's, Fantic sports mopeds, C.Z. Motorcycles and Garella sports mopeds. Vespas generated a lot of income through the workshop with repairs, such as the front fork pin sets, wheel bearings, clutches, replacement of the cush drive springs, main bearings, barrel and pistons, more so on the smaller 50cc models.

On all new sales, we gave away a free bottle of Filtrate two-stroke oil to try and help the customer, and stop them seizing up in the running in periods and beyond.

A lot of extra work was created for the workshop by converting the smaller 50cc models to 90cc when the customer passed their test. We modified the carburettor and silencer. When carrying out this modification, it gave a much higher speed. Our sales of Jawa/CZ motorcycles were good which qualified us to go on a free dealer's trip to Czechoslovakia.

Around this time, Terry Shea sold the shop back to Roy Cary as he was still the lease holder of the premises. Doug May and myself would carry on running the shop with Peter Blackburn until the shop closed 1984.

TRIP TO PRAGUE CZECHOSLOVAKIA 1982

I was lucky enough to go on the free dealer trip for five days, along with 20 other dealers, to the Jawa/CZ factory.

We set off from London Airport on Thursday 17th October and arrived at Prague Airport at 4.30 p.m. We were staying at the large, modern International Hotel.

Our first day there we travelled by coach to Motokov premises for lunch at their Head Offices, which was around 20 stories high. We had a fantastic view while eating our lunch; afterwards we visited a Technical Museum.

The following day was spent sight-seeing by coach around Prague and then on to an Aeronautical Museum. They liked showing off their museums.

We also went to see the final round of the European Autocross Championship. The coach returned us to our hotel for dinner, after a good wash to get rid of all the dust we acquired from watching the racing.

On our final day, we had another long coach ride to visit the Velorex factory that made all the sidecars for JAWA/CZ bikes, followed by a barbecue and drinks at the Holiday Centre and then back to our hotel ready for our return home the following day.

I would like to say a very big thank you to all the CZ representatives that came with us on the memorial visit to Prague. I had a great time and found it extremely interesting.

A general view of Prague from high up on the Hill.

Everyone was invited to a barbeque at the holiday centre where all the CZ workers went; from the top boss down to the man that cleaned the floors.

November 1984 saw the shop close its doors for the last time. We were now unemployed. The photograph shows some of our customers that turned up on our last day and gave us a signed card to wish us all the best. I must say it did help to lift a heavy heart.

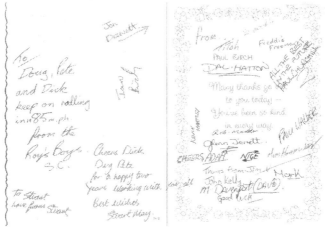

RESTORATION

I purchased this little Vespa 50 in 1984; it was an insurance right-off. The engine had seized and the rider fell off bending the forks and damaging the body work, and front mudguard. Not a big job. It was soon repaired and back on the road ready for my youngest daughter Debbie to ride. She did not like the colour and wanted more speed so this would be my first restoration project away from work. I fitted a 90cc kit to the engine and re-sprayed the scooter in mini flake red, all from spray cans. Jan made the seat and back rest cover.

My youngest daughter Debbie on my GP 125 LAMBRETTA She was
thinking of having this machine, but bought a car instead.

I purchased this GP 125 Lambretta from Paul Hughes from Hornchurch, Essex in October 1983, for one hundred and twenty pounds. The machine had been sprayed, but was not put together. The fibre glass panels were cut away and the clutch cover had been chromed. There was no saddle or stand feet and many other little pieces missing. Tom, my eldest daughter Stephanie's husband purchased this machine from me as he needed transport for work and eventually he sold it to Kegra Scooters in Southend, Essex.

SCOOTER RESTORATIONS

When working on a scooter restoration, I followed the same procedure as I did when I worked for Lambretta Concessionaires Limited. The machine and engine were washed down, which made it much nicer to work on, plus it made the scooter look better when the work was completed. Once the scooter was stripped down and re-sprayed, I fitted new rubbers to the stand and fitted it to the frame.

Next, I made up the front forks, and fitted the steering bearings to the frame. Then I fitted the forks and front wheel and placed a support under the rear frame. Next the saddle and side panel rubbers were fitted to the frame. This was done to stop any damage to the paint work. Next to be fitted were the lower handlebars to the forks, toolbox lid, petrol lid, choke control, rear lamp body and all the controls into the handlebars. Finally, I fitted all the cables and loom plus the horn and HT coil.

The engine was next to be fitted, without the rear hub, so now all the cables were connected along with the loom to the rectifier, HT coil and rear lamp. I then fitted the toolbox and the petrol tank, air filter box, number plate, rear panel catches and rear mudguard, and then rear hub and wheel. I always fitted the leg shields together with the rear footboards to make sure they all lined up with no gaps. Next to be fitted were the front mudguard and horn casting then the rear brake pedal and stop light switch. Lastly, I fitted the handlebar top and headlamp, and the handles to the panels, if they had them.

Job done apart from starting it up and making sure everything worked and checked the final adjustments.

NEW SHOP OWNER

Alan Pritchard of Alspeed Performance Limited, London Road, Southend-on-Sea, Essex was the distributor for the Spanish Lambretta, and took over the Roy's of Hornchurch shop trading as Enterprise Motorcycles, along with Mike Karslake. Roy wanted to concentrate on his imported Fantic Motors which were selling very well.

Not long after this, Mike moved to Devon to set up his museum. I was approached by Alan and Mike to run the shop. I turned the offer down, and suggested they ask Doug May. Doug took up the offer and ran the shop until Alan wanted to call it a day. I believe Doug ran the shop on his own for some time, but in the end the shop went back into Roy's hands as he was still the lease holder. Roy was now into electric motor toys. I believe this came about because Fantic Motors in Italy stopped production of their motorcycles.

The shop was renamed Classic Chassis and moved to new premises in Upminster, Essex, during 2010.

For my part I have not stopped working with Lambretta and Vespas and have helped quite a few people with their restorations until I retired. Now I look after my own scooters.

Kelly Langley's GS 150 Vespa before a complete restoration was carried out.

CHAPTER 14
40TH ANNIVERSARY OF INNOCENTI LAMBRETTA SCOOTERS 1987 MIKE KARSLAKES SCOOTER MUSEUM

Another trip to Northlew, Devon was to attend the 40th Anniversary of Innocenti Lambretta scooters, organised by Mike. A great many Lambretta members and some staff from the concessionaires attended this great event.

This plaque was made by Rachel, Mike's wife, to celebrate the anniversary.

Photograph showing from left to right. Mr Bennett — Original Service Manager. Mr P J Agg — Managing Director. Mr Baker — Dispatch Manager. Mrs. Calder — Mr. Agg's Secretary and Director of the firm. Bob Wilkinson — General Secretary L.C.G.B.

40th ANNIVERSARY OF INNOCENTI LAMBRETTA SCOOTERS

Chuck Swonnal on the left, Dick Beal one of the technical
representatives right and Dick Sedgley in the middle.

Mike and Dick Sedgley in his museum; unfortunately, I cannot
remember the name of the person in the middle.

Photographs of Mike's museum, his pride and joy — all looking very smart.

EPSOM 'WHIRLWINDS' SCOOTER CLUB MEMBERS
Visit to Mike's Lambretta museum in 1989.

From left to right Mike Smallbone, Dick Sedgley, Dot Howard, Tom Howard and Margaret Smallbone. We had a very interesting day and a good chat with Mike once again. Little did I know this would be the last time I would see him.

Left to right: Jan Sedgley, Tom Howard and Dot Howard standing beside Mike's Lambretta fire engine.

MIKE KARSLAKE 1932—1990

Mike Karslake sadly passed away from a heart attack in 1990. It was a very sad day and a great loss to all involved with Lambretta scooters. Rachel held Mike's funeral in the village at Northlew, Devon and the village was packed with scooters, friends and family.

AUCTION OF MIKE'S MUSEUM — 1991

Having celebrated Mike's life at the local church in Northlew, Devon in 1990 we are back again for the auction of Mike's museum.

This was a very sad time for Jan and I and our thoughts were with Rachel and her family after the loss of a very good friend.

The photograph shows just a small part of what was going to be sold. The TV 175 Series I in the photograph was what Mike was planning to build at the same time as myself. This was the machine I built the engine for, and when both the scooters were completed we were planning a long trip together.

Our third and last trip to Northlew.

CHAPTER 15
MY FIRST RESTORATION OF MY OWN

Below is a 1958 TV 175 Series I, which Mike Karslake gave to me for all the help I gave him when setting up the Lambretta Preservation Society.

As you can see, it was in a very poor state and took hours of work to put right. First, I made a list of all the parts required. That was the easy part; the hard part was to obtain the parts needed for this restoration project. The main parts being a complete front and rear hub, wheel rims tyres, tubes, a complete stand and fittings, right-hand footboard, saddle, rear carrier, head lamp, major repair to leg shields, and rear part of frame. It would be quite a few years before this Lambretta was back on the road.

I decided not to start the restoration until I had all the parts needed to do the job. It was at this point I phoned Mike Karslake to see how he was getting on with his TV 175 Series I, and whether he could help me with some parts that I needed. Mike was hard at work with his museum, but I paid him a visit.

Mike asked me to re-condition his engine for him, in exchange for my labour and all the new parts fitted he would give me some spares for my engine and some other parts I needed, which was a great help. However, I still needed quite a few other bits. I obtained some from a dealer in Southend,

Horner's of Manchester and a dealer in London near where I was working at the time.

Mike's engine was repaired so this would be my second trip to Devon and once again a good look around the museum and much talk about the good old days!

RESTORING OLD LAMBRETTA SCOOTERS SAD LOSS OF MIKE KARSLAKE — 1990

After the sad loss of Mike, I lost interest in working on the TV 175 Series I for a while, but eventually I made a start on the scooter again.

I was still short of two side panels and a front mudguard. My luck changed when I received a telephone call from an old friend Melvyn Barefoot who wanted to sell his TV 175 Series I that had been restored. He only wanted £700.00 for it as he had sold the engine and rear damper to Peter Wells. He ran the scooter with a TV 175 Series II engine in it for a while before selling the scooter to me. So, at last, I knew I had all the parts to make one good scooter.

I had taken the mudguard and leg shields off Melvyn's scooter when I noticed the paint work was starting to bubble up and the inside of the left-hand panel was very bad. This was not Melvyn's fault as he paid a lot of money for the scooter to be restored.

I paint stripped all the metal parts on my TV 175 Series I, which took me ten and half hours to complete — never again; shot blasting in future! The frame work took the longest time, as under the first coat of green was brown, then blue, then red and at last down to original coat of cream.

A further six and three quarter hours was spent cutting out sheet metal to fabricate parts for the rear frame grill, right-hand footboard, rear inner mudguard and the right hand panel, where Melvyn had cut a section out above the kick start pedal for his Series II engine. Three and a half hours were spent making two stand brackets to weld to the frame and the second to hold the stand in place. Twelve hours were spent repairing the silencer, a large hole the size of a golf ball was where the tail pipe used to be.

Everything inside the box had rotted away; the body of the silencer was in fair condition. I cut the silencer in half and made all new baffles and pipes, welded them in place, and put the silencer back together. I made a complete new main bracket, plus I repaired the rear end of the silencer to take the tail pipe, which I also had made plus a new bracket.

My thanks go to my other son-in-law, Martin Childs, for all the welding work done on this scooter.

Twenty-two hours were spent on cleaning off about forty years of dirt and corrosion from the engine, removing a much seized barrel and piston, plus the exhaust ring on the barrel. I removed six broken studs, reconditioned the stator plate, plus new loom, contacts, condenser and flywheel re-magnetised. I removed the seized brake cam and brake shoes, reconditioned the carburettor, made up all new gaskets from gasket paper. All new bearings and oil seals fitted, plus a new crankshaft, reamed out small end bush, re-bored barrel and piston, new clutch plates, springs and new chain.

The repair to rear of frame.

304

The TV 175 Series I that I purchased from Melvyn Barfoot without the engine, rear damper and right-hand rear footboard. The paint work looks very good in this photograph.

Some of the rust that was just sprayed over!!

My second grandson James helped to remove the rust from Melvyn's leg shields after we stripped the paint off.

Showing a very dirty engine, something like 40 years' worth of dirt!

The engine casings were all clean and bright, plus the entire engine parts. All new bearings and oil seals fitted, barrel re-

bored, stator plate and carburettor over hauled. All I had to do now was to remember how it all went back together, after putting the engine together, I treated all metal body parts with Kill Rust.

It is now March 1998 and the weather is starting to get a little warmer so I set about spraying the scooter. Any metal parts that needed it were treated with Rust Kill. I sprayed all the metal parts with red lead and applied the under seal to all parts that had under seal on the original scooter. I made a spray booth out of timber and plastic sheeting and sprayed everything in a light grey under coat, then the cream coats.

Red lead done now for the underseal.

My ultra-modern spray booth! I had a lot of hair when I first started on
this scooter!

Finally, the coffee coats, my luck held out as the weather was
good all week. The spray work came out really good. This was
my first attempt at spraying with a compressor and gun, and it
would be my last. From now on most of my spray work would
be done by Andy in Crow Lane, Romford, Essex. The time
spent building the spray booth, spraying the parts and clearing
up took forty-nine hours and a further forty-six and three
quarters of an hour was spent cleaning all parts to be refitted.
This included the Speedo head, polishing all aluminium parts
and making up complete cables with oilers, and putting it all
back together. Next, I road tested it and made any final
adjustments. A trip to the MOT station took up a further three
hours. In total of one hundred and fifty hours thirty minutes on
this scooter from scrap to a sparkling scooter. Other costs
involved many telephone calls, postage and travelling by car
to pick up spares.

Below are my two eldest grandsons Sam and James. What was it I said: do not sit on the scooter when it is on the stand?

All ready for my trip to Southend from London.

JUNE 2000

At long last, I am on the road with my TV 175 Series I. The last time I rode this type of model was back in 1959 when I traded in my two year old LDB 150 Mark 2½ for a brand new TV 175 Series I in coffee and cream colours.

My first trip out was on the London ride out, despite the cold damp start to the day. It felt great to be back riding the scooter again.

It was a slow ride to and from Southend, Essex as I was running in the scooter, and parts of my body were glad to get back home and into a soft chair and have a hot cup of tea.

The scooter ran extremely well and never missed a beat, which I was very happy about.

The Half-Way House pub stop on our way to Southend.

2001 On my second London ride out Jan came with me. The photograph was taken at the Half-Way stop on the A127. The pub is no longer there; in its place, there is a big block of flats.

2002 On my third London ride out to Southend, I met up with Chuck Swonnell on his Vespa. As you can see from the photograph it was a very sunny day. We enjoyed a good old chat about past times and people we have met from years gone by.

DICK SEDGLEY'S HOME MADE HYDRAULIC WORK BENCH

This hydraulic bed was given to me by Christine Jackson. I believe it was some sort of hospital bed; you can see the pedal to raise or lower the wheels.

The top was cut off; also the two main supports were cut down to lower the bed as much as possible. All paint and rust removed. A complete new top frame made and welded to the hydraulic base, and sprayed in white primer.

The bench is 27 inches wide x 78 inches long x 14 inches high when fully down. The ramp hooks onto the end of the bench and is 9½ inches wide and 51 inches long. A quarter of an inch ply board, cut ready to fit now. The spraying is completed in Lambretta blue. I have three Series III wiring diagrams on the wall to the right of the ramp.

The lacquered ply board was fitted to the very good looking ramp. In full working condition the ramp stands 34 inches high.

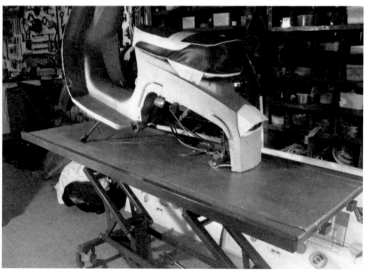

Aluminium sheeting was fitted on top of plywood for protection and at last it was in full working order. The Starstream scooter on the ramp is waiting to be restored.

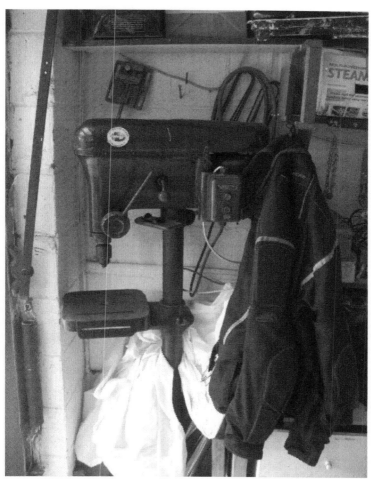

My six foot pillar drill. Most handy as a coat hanger too. The hydraulic ramp was much better for me as it is easy to move around, unlike the big red ramp I had before with no wheels. My thanks go to John Roberts for supplying all the metal and my son-in-law Martin for doing all the welding once again.

SECOND TV 175 SERIES I RESTORATION

I was so pleased with the way my TV 175 Series I had performed, my thoughts turned to what I had left: a good frame, forks and a lot of other pieces.

By chance I called into see Doug May who was still running the shop in Hornchurch and to my great surprise he was able to supply me with two side panels, front mudguard and leg shields; they were in a poor state, but were better than the ones I had.

I also obtained a very old dual seat from Pete Maisey from the Companions Scooter Club. All I needed now were quite a few engine parts.

Once again, I called Peter Wells who said he could help if I would like to call over to see him, which I did as soon as possible. After a chat and a cup of tea, we moved to his workshop and sat on his bench was the TV 175 Series I engine he had bought from Melvyn Barfoot. A deal was struck there and then. To say I was pleased with the outcome goes without saying.

We are now good friends and whenever I go to see Peter there is always a lunch supplied and plenty of chatting about scooters.

So now I could start to build my second TV 175 Series I. This was the later model; no adjusters on the handlebars, no slots cut in the panels, a much larger rectifier and a different wiring loom. It had the same tank and petrol tap as the TV 175 Series II and had holes in the frame where the air scoop was fitted for Series II 175 models.

The photo shows all the paint removed from metal parts, with most of the welding completed, apart from the right-hand footboard, which has a piece cut out of it for some reason. A lot of these metal parts would be treated with Kill Rust before red lead spraying followed by a light grey under coat applied.

I had no paint left, thank goodness, and all my spray work would be farmed out from now on, including this time. It would be sprayed in black and red with a gold outline.

Pete Maisey gave me the saddle but it still cost me about £90.00 to have it repaired and re-covered.

My son-in-law, Martin, did all the welding for me once again to which I was most grateful.

This was the engine I bought from Peter Wells and was unsure of how many miles it had done. It was stripped down, which was just as well, as the flywheel needed to be re-magnetised and the crankshaft was not too good. I had a new conrod fitted by Ray at A.F. Rayspeed. The barrel re-bored and a new piston, new chain, all new bearings and oil seals, new clutch plates, plus a new exhaust box and pipe from Patch in West London.

The inner workings of a TV 175 Series I engine.

The old silencer that had seen better days.

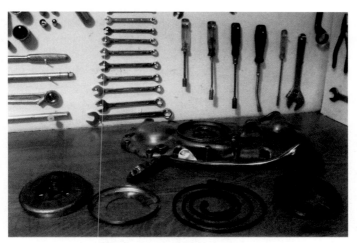

Clutch cover and kick-start parts.

'Job done', in the same colours I had sprayed way back in 1959 by
Lambretta Concessionaires in Wimbledon SW19.

I received a telephone call from Peter Wells wanting to know
if I would like to restore another TV 175 Series I. The
gentleman's name was Martin Whittaker and he lived a fair
distance away, but he would be willing to bring the scooter to

me. I agreed. The photograph shows no engine or front mudguard at first glance. This scooter would require a lot of work.

Martin went to the Lambretta Museum at Weston-super-Mare, Somerset, and bought a complete engine, front mudguard and loads of other pieces. He then made the journey to my house to deliver the parts.

A layer of fibre glass was used on the leg shields in place of the rubber mats. On removing the fibreglass, it revealed a lot of rust plus a few holes. This would have to be repaired along with other body parts.

The engine was completely over-hauled; the body work was very rusty in places. After the bead blasting was finished, welding and panel beating was next. I applied a coat of red lead paint after a coat of Kill Rust to all metal parts. Then the scooter was taken to Andy's in Crow Lane, Romford, Essex to be sprayed in its original colours of coffee and cream. Once it was all back together, I had trouble starting the engine. It turned out the flywheel was no good. Martin made a further trip to the Lambretta Museum to buy another flywheel.

Once the second flywheel was fitted to the machine, it started up straight away and ran very well, thank goodness, as this restoration turned out to be very costly. This scooter is still being used on the road to date.

Scooter before and after.

TV 175 Series I Handbook

A copy of the handbook supplied with your new scooter. It gave all the servicing and running-in details. A wiring loom diagram, lubrication chart, a guide to assist in the tracing of faults if the scooter stopped or would not start and a list of all the Main Dealers in the UK.

Each scooter had a good tool roll kit with a rear stand to lift the scooter up if you had to change the rear wheel.

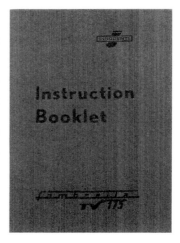

MY NEXT SCOOTER RESTORATION

Jan's original LI 150 Lambretta Series I was red/white and she had it re-sprayed yellow/black in 1961. This LI 150 Series I was restored in yellow/black. My younger daughter Debbie, Jan, and our younger grandchildren Michaela and Luke.

I like my little Vespa now, but when can I have my proper scooter.

MY NEXT RESTORATION

My next restoration came about via Peter Wells; he needed some work done on one of his scooters. In return, he gave me this LDB 150 as he did not want to do another restoration.

The scooter only had 24,000 miles on the clock and one owner. The owner fell off it one day and never rode it again. It was left in the back garden and was just rusting away until he passed away. His wife then sold it to Peter without the log book as she was unable to find it.

The corrosion was very bad on all the metal parts. The engine kicked over so I cleaned the contacts, carburettor and plug, put some petrol in a spare tank and it started after a few kicks. I was about to try the gears when the bottom of the silencer blew out so that was that. The next step was to strip it all down. Thank goodness the engine was covered in oil; you do not often say that. When the engine was finally cleaned up it looked really good.

I wanted to use all the original parts if I could, but this was not possible in the end. After having the machine shot blasted, the leg shields, front wheel rims, and both rear footboards were unusable. The top of the petrol tank was full of holes, as were the front mudguard. A good repair was carried out on them.

The engine was stripped down after a major clean up. The only new parts needed were bearings, oil seals, gaskets and clutch plates. The barrel and piston were in good condition as were the crankshaft. All I had to do was fit a new small end bush which says a great deal about the engineering that went into making these Lambretta scooters.

The scooter would be a duplicate of the scooter I purchased in 1957 and would have white panels and sides of the front mudguard. The rest of the scooter was sprayed in the original blue colour, as it was in 1957 for this model LDB 150

Mark 2½.

My thanks to Christine Jackson for taking me and the scooter in her van to Sidcup, Kent to have the machine registered and receive a new age related number plate because I never had a log book with the scooter.

My thanks to Patch at Scooter Surgery, Hammersmith, London W6 7PP for many parts purchased over the last few years and a special thank you to Mauld who is always happy and willing to help.

At last, I was on the road after having the machine registered and MOT.

I have since had the engine stripped out twice to replace rubbish oil seals that went soft and distorted in the petrol oil mix. I have since found out other people have suffered this problem also.

My thanks to Cambridge Lambretta, 95 Ditton Walk, Stepneys Yard, Cambridge for supplying top quality oil seals solving the problem.

Original state of the scooter.

From one pile of rusted metal and bad back ache too

The finished LDB 150 Mark 2½ Lambretta scooter. 1957 vintage

MY LAST RESTORATION

This would be my fifth and last restoration to date. This scooter originated from Enterprise Motorcycles in 1978 where it was sold to a Mr S Martin, who lived about two miles from the shop in Hornchurch. He had traded in his old LI 150 Lambretta for £50.00 for a new GP 150.

This was our first Indian 150 sold in the shop. A lot of the engine parts were from The Innocenti factory. It also had a Dellorto carburettor fitted. The paint work was very good, as you can see in the picture below. Mr Martin had his panels nicked the first day he rode it to work in London. He decided to have an old pair of panels so we sold him a pair of GT 200 panels for about £10.00.

A 27-year-old GP 150 — paintwork still in good condition apart from the panels — Mileage 34,917.

Mr Martin was a good customer and we became friends over the years, even after the shop closed. So it was no surprise to me when Sonny telephoned me to ask if I could call around to look at his scooter.

The big surprise came when he told me he wanted to sell the scooter as he was unable to ride it anymore, and would I like to buy it, which I did for £250.00.

LAMBRETTA SCOOTER WMP 565T
SOLD TO RICHARD SEDELEY FOR £250
SOLD AS SEEN 8.11.05.

Below is the original sales invoice from Enterprise Motorcycles.

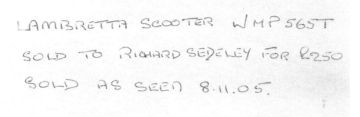

Once again, if I had known how much this restoration was going to cost me at the start, I think I would have left it as it was because it was running quite well, although it needed two new tyres, and I did not like the look of the old GT 200 panels.

I stripped the machine down to see what was needed. I started with the engine. The barrel and piston were OK. The crankshaft was showing signs of wear, as were the bearings, so they were replaced along with the clutch plates, springs and chain.

Next I stripped down all the body work ready for bead blasting and made a list of all the parts needed. It was at this point, I thought I would like to make this scooter into a Royspeed 150.

Luckily, the cylinder was a proper Innocenti type so not too much work was needed to make it into a Royspeed barrel. All the engine parts, side panels and black trim came from A.F. Rayspeed along with other parts including tyres and tubes. I had a spare disc brake which I decided to use. The damper brackets were welded to the forks so even more spares were needed, such as new fork links, springs and dampers. I modified the disc brake to the same standard as I had on my TV 175 III when I was racing all those years ago.

The colour would be metallic blue with silver hubs and forks. Once again it will be sprayed by Andy in Crow Lane, Romford.

I fitted all new aluminium parts to the handlebars, horn grill, and rear frame grill and also fitted a new Italian GP rear lamp. These parts were obtained from Scooter Restoration, Nottingham.

I also fitted a new headlamp, ignition switch, dip switch, speedo head and all badges to leg shields and horn casting. The saddle was re-covered and a sprint rack was fitted to the rear. A spare wheel and carrier were fitted to the leg shields. The original number plate was fitted back and the Royspeed stickers were put on the panels. Once again after an MOT my first long trip out was the London ride to Southend. It was some time after I decided to make the GP into a 200cc as  I had already changed the magneto to a Rayspeed lightweight 12 volt system. All I needed now was a 200 crankcase, sprockets and chain, plus by now a new bank manager. I must thank John Roberts for the Royspeed panel stickers.

Finished GP 150/200 next to all my restored scooters.

The time will come when they will be for sale.

It took me all day to clean and polish all these scooters which was nothing compared to all the time spent on the restorations. I do not talk about the cost involved in getting these scooters back on the road. Since this photo was taken, I have sold the yellow and black LI 150 Series I, also the coffee and cream series I TV175. The Royspeed GP200 will be the next to go.

My five restored Lambretta scooters. All have been ridden on the road at some time after being restored.

1957 LDB 150 Mark 2½ original colour mid blue
1959 LI 150 Series I original colour red/white — now yellow and black
1958 TV 175 Series I original colour coffee/cream
1959 TV 175 Series I original colour coffee/cream — now red and black
GP 150/200 original colour mid blue — now a Royspeed mini flake blue

THE COVENTRY VINTAGE MOTOR SCOOTER CLUB SHOW 2009

It started with a telephone call from Christine Jackson, asking if I would I like to do the Coventry show with her? In the end, I agreed. The theme would be a dealers showroom in 1957. As we both had restored LDBs and D' from that year Christine and her friend Terry Ball made the shop frame and painted it. Jan, my wife, sorted out all the posters and literature to go on the outside of the shop walls. I supplied the dealers signs, oil drum, and repainted the scooter stands. After many hours of hard work we were ready to go. The shop was flat packed and would have to be constructed at the show. All this had to fit in Christine's van and our car. This would be quite a job getting ready for the show on time. Apart from Christine, Jan and myself we also had help, thank goodness, from David Jackson, Christine's nephew and Doug Miller a veteran of many years on a Lambretta.

We won 'Best Stand' at the show much to our delight after all our hard work. Unfortunately, Graham Bird another veteran of many years scootering was unable to help this year.

Christine obtained quite a few scooter banners for displaying in the shop from Chuck Swonnell to which we were most grateful as it added to our shop display of the 1950s when scooter clubs were in full swing.

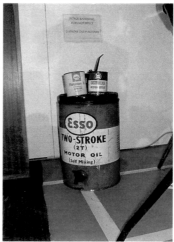

Grease and two-stroke oils a dealer would have in his workshop.

My Mark 2½ LDB 150 sprayed in the colours of my original new LDB 150 in 1957.

An illuminated Lambretta sign, and on the counter a black telephone and Pirelli Tyre Ashtray.

Showing the display of a Dealer Showroom in 1957 displayed at the Coventry V.M.S.C. show 2009. Designed by Christine Jackson and with me thinking I could do with a nice cold beer.

On display in the shop Dick's 1957 LDB 150 Mark 2½ and Christine's 1957 LDB 150 Mark III.

My wife Jan's Bush Radio with Christine Jackson's black telephone and Italian coffee pot with cups on the coffee table I made at school.

CHAPTER 16
EPSOM 'WHIRLWINDS' SCOOTER CLUB RE-UNIONS 30TH ANNIVERSARY

Our first scooter club re-union after 30 years was held in a hall of the Epsom Gas Board Club.

There were many excited members and many handshakes plus a lot of laughter mixed with scooter talk. It was fantastic to all get together again. We arranged to meet again at some time in the future.

Photo below shows our members before they left for that evening, promising to keep in touch.

WHIRLWINDS' SCOOTER CLUB 50TH ANNIVERSARY

On Saturday 7th January 2007, our scooter club celebrated their 50th anniversary at the Kings Arm pub, East Street, Epsom, Surrey. We arranged to meet about 4pm, and the room was crowded almost immediately. John Wood and I had managed to put all the memorabilia and photographs out earlier.

We expected about 23 old club members who had previously booked a meal from Tony, the chef and owner of the pub. The buzz in the separate bar area was great, even the locals were inquisitive.

Memories flew around the room, with hearty handshakes, hugs and much laughter. We had an unexpected guest Chuck Swonnell, whom was most welcome and we managed to order him a meal.

Everybody left late that evening promising to meet again sooner rather than later. Many of us met the following day at Tony's Pub for a farewell drink.

Chuckles enjoying himself talking to some of our club members.

Photograph taken by Chuck Swonnell sometime during the evening.

COLLIER ROW, ROMFORD PARTS FAIR AND SHOW.

Dick's 1957 LDB 150 Mark 2½ on display at Collier Row Parts Fair and Scooter Show organised by two local scooter clubs in Hornchurch called 'The F.A.B.s' and 'The Specials'.

The theme of the display was the 50th Anniversary of Epsom Whirlwinds Scooter Club — 2007.

I was very lucky with my display of the 50th anniversary with the Epsom Lambretta Club. I won 'Best Ridden Scooter' in the show, and 'Best Scooter' in the show, as voted by the public. To say I was very pleased would not be an understatement. Plus, it was a very good day out and also supported by our local scooter shop 'Ricky Pit Stop'. We still have four members of the Epsom Lambretta Club riding scooters. Peter Simmons, Steve Brunt, John Wood and myself.

Other events held by The Specials Scooter Club are Easter egg runs and family days, where everybody can show off their scooters and have a good time. Some of the members of these clubs go back to the days of Roy's of Hornchurch. Alan Malony being one of them and Mark Davenport; unfortunately, I cannot remember everyone's name. Sorry.

53rd EPSOM SCOOTER CLUB ANNIVERSARY — 2010
RUBBING HOUSE, EPSOM DOWNS

Lunchtime in the Rubbing House. All the talk of scooters made me thirsty.

Epsom Lambretta Club members that were able to make this years' get together on the Epsom Downs Racecourse.

EPSOM LAMBRETTA CLUB 2011

The club is in its 54th year and we met on Epsom Downs for lunch in the Rubbing House once again. We hoped that the members that were unable to make it last year, would attend this time.

LONDON RIDE OUT SOUTHEND-ON-SEA, ESSEX.

This was the last London Ride out I would attend and was a good test for my second TV175 Series I. The weather was good which made it a great day out. The ride from London was something to see, if you were able to actually see through the blue haze of two stroke smoke! It was so good to reach Southend and take in some nice sea air.

John Wood on his red/black GP 225. Standing in front of Dick's red/black TV 175 Series I is Jay, who always goes on the London Ride out with us. His partner Helen also came along on some of the local scooter club runs.

EPSOM WHIIRLWINDS SCOOTER CLUB REUNION 2012

Rubbing House pub, Epsom Downs, Surrey having a cup of coffee while waiting for other members to arrive.

CLUB REUNION 2013

After lunch photograph with the grandstand in the background. We had two guests with us, Barbara and Peter Pooley from Cheam Scooter Club.

CRICKETERS PUB — WEST HILL, EPSOM, SURREY
SCOOTER CLUB REUNION 2014

The pub where we held our first meeting as a brand new scooter club, way back in the 1950s and 57 years later we were back. The pond, trees and bushes make a lovely backdrop whilst having lunch. Barbara and Peter Poolev with Steve Brunt.

Far left, John Wood with Crash helmet talking to Chris Mitchell (not in photo) with Steve Brunt and Janet Sedgley looking on. Dick Sedgley talking to customer in the pub who was very interested in our scooters and was amazed at the condition of them. He needed another pint after we told him how much they were to restore!

Peter Simmons with his restored GP 200. He has been a member of the
Epsom Whirlwinds since the 1960's. All his scooters are maintained to
a very high standard.

John Wood and Steve Brunt all long term members of the Epsom Club
talking to people interested in the scooters.

CRICKETERS PUB, WEST HILL, EPSOM, SURREY
REUNION 2015

From left to right of photograph. John Wood, Peter Pooley, Dick
Sedgley, Chris Mitchell, Barbara Pooley, Mervyn Sedgley and Shelia
and Peter Ward.

Steve Brunt's restored Orange RB 250; the machine started its life as a
TV 175 Series III in 1962. Best not to ask how much it cost!

CHAPTER 17
STINGRAY PROJECT 2012
for Christine Jackson

Looking a little sad after many years of neglect.

It does not look any better the other side.

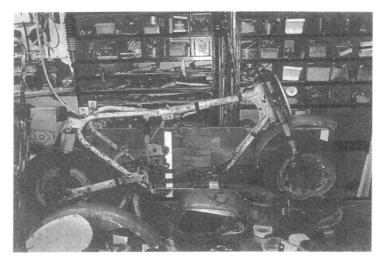

The start of many hours of work.

Crankcase and clutch cover before and after quite a few hours of work.

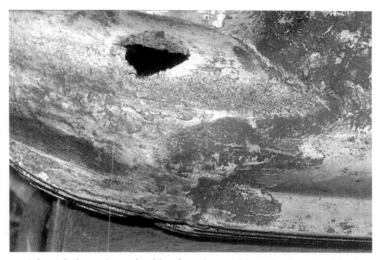

A large hole on the underside of crankcase. this took a lot of welding and making good.

Picture showing drive side oil seal and retaining plate covered in some sort of filler to improve gas flow.

Rear view of crankcase showing the ridge removed to stop the engine coming into contact with the frame.

The clutch cover showing aluminium repair that was to be ground down to give clearance for the front sprocket.

The main crankcase showing the parts that were welded together. This also had to be ground down as the chain was rubbing against it. Four studs also had to be replaced.

Clutch cover showing kick start face machined down ready to be drilled and tapped to take four retaining bolts securing the oil seal and plate.

Engine parts all cleaned and ready to be refitted. Barrel was re-bored and fitted with new piston. You can see this barrel has a bridged exhaust.

Picture of modified exhaust all welded up and derusted ready to be sprayed in silver. You can also see some of the bolts welded to the silencer to fix the heat shield.

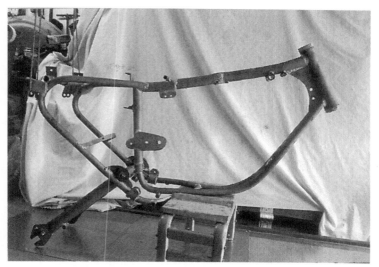

Frame after shot blasting and painted in Kill RustFive hours spent making a robust centre stand out of steel tube and wood to rest the bike on to carry out this restoration project.

Front engine bracket support re-brazed along with re-brazing of front fork legs.

Repaired and re-brazed rear brake pedal brackets also top engine bracket on the main down tube.

All the holes in the cylinder head were elongated to make it fit the Lambretta 200 Barrel studs. Bella 200 Cylinder head repair. Spark plug location was refaced along with all the cylinder head stud holes, plus the gasket surface was refaced.

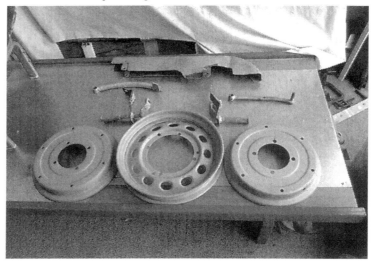

All the metal parts were shot blasted and checked over for any defects.

All parts were sprayed in red lead and topcoat of white or blue. The two footrests had to be repaired then painted black. Ten and a half hours spent spraying in red lead, white undercoat then white or blue top coast. Chain guard footrest in black.

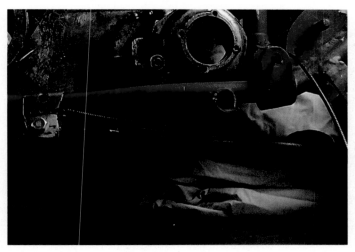

All metal parts were shot blasted, repaired and welded where necessary and sprayed in red lead paint, primer coat and white topcoat. The picture also shows the temporary bracket to fix the side stand and spring.

This picture shows the remade battery carrier and bracket bolted to the frame. The two remade battery straps will be fixed to each end and a rubber mat fitted to protect the battery.

Painted parts all ready for fitting after some had to be repaired and welded. All the hubs, mudguards, and petrol tank were sprayed in blue. Modified rear chain guard welded and sprayed black.

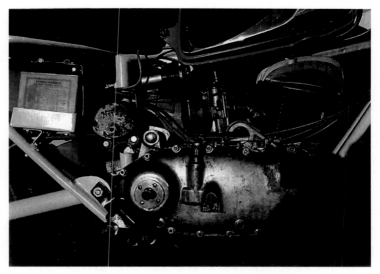

Photo showing battery in place and just to the right the Norton foot gear change mechanism. Just below that you can see the oil seal retaining plate fitted to the kick start shaft.

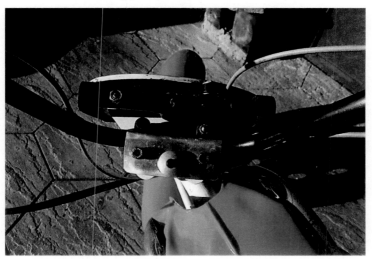

Photo showing LI Series I cut out button mounted on an aluminium plate fixed to the handlebars.

Photo showing complete scooter with LD handlebar gear change, aluminium steering stops on bottom, fork yoke, flywheel cover and exhaust with heat protection grills and side stand.

Front view of completed Stingray 200 with new tyre and fork gaiters.

Rear view of completed Stingray 200 with new saddle cover and new rear shock absorbers.

Right-hand view of completed Stingray 200 showing modified engine casing to take hand gear change parts. The modified kick-start pedal was rubbing on the aluminium kick start pedal stop on the clutch cover, so it was removed. An aluminium plate and gasket had to be made to cover the hole in the case. This was held in place with four fixing screws.

A big smile — completed at last.

One hundred and seventeen hours in total spent on reconditioning two engines, stripping down and rebuilding the scooter; making and modifying parts to make this machine up to road standard, for a daylight MOT test.

My thanks go to Tony Hickmott for his help and advice on the Stingray, plus making a very good kick-start pedal for this machine. Plus sending the motorcycle books of me carrying out service repairs for Lambretta Concessionaries at Croydon.

Also, thanks to my son-in-law Martin Childs who completed all the welding.

TRIBUTE TO JOHN TAYLOR

The last time I saw John Taylor's 'YELLOW PERIL' Lambretta was at the Comax Rally at Bedfords Park, Romford, Essex back in the early seventies run by the Companions Scooter Club.

He was one of the top riders on grass track events back in the sixties.

I completed the Stingray restoration just in time for the Bats Scooter Club reunion scramble meeting and rally, June 2013, for Christine Jackson.

John Taylor called in to see me on his way to the rally as he wanted to have his flywheel re-magnetised, as he was having trouble starting his scooter. Once it was fixed, we had a cup of tea and a good old chat about the past.

I saw him next day at the Scramble meeting and his scooter was working well. Little did I know this would be the last time I would see him alive. A few weeks later he sadly passed away quite suddenly. It was a great shock to Jan and me and our thoughts are still with Shelia and family.

RAY COLLINS' MEMORIAL 2015 ELSTEAD ROYAL COMMON, SURREY

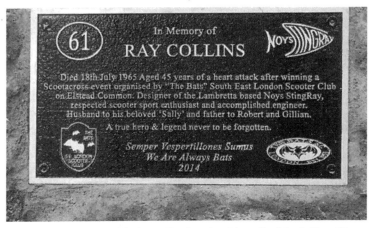

Ray Collins' memorial plaque fixed to the side wall of the bridge. The racetrack ran over the bridge.

Christine Jackson holding the Stingray while the chain and rear brake are adjusted.

ELSTEAD ROYAL COMMON, SURREY 2015

Peter Pooley of Cheam Cheeters and the GT 200 Lambretta Club
testing his skills on the track.

John Wood of Epsom Whirlwinds Scooter Club having a great time
riding No. 15.

Dick Sedgley Epsom Whirlwinds Scooter Club. Having a great time riding the Stingray at Elstead, having spent many hours restoring it.

Six competitors getting ready to complete four laps of the scramble track.

Andy Gillard giving No. 61 a try out before letting Ann his partner ride it around the scramble track with the other competitors. Our thanks to Barry and his pals for running the event and Christine Jackson for bringing her Stingray machines.

After packing everything up and scooters back on trailers we made a dash to The Mill pub in Elstead for lunch and judging by all the talk at the table a good time was had by all present at this event.

50th ANNIVERARY OF RAYSPEED 'S' TYPE LAMBRETTA EVENT 15/16/17 AUGUST 2014

Dick Sedgley, Ray Kemp and Haydon Redfern. Are these the three original musketeers?

Best model at the show. No, not the GP that came a close second to my wife, Jan.

AF RAYSPEED 15/16/17 AUGUST 2015

I was very pleased to be one of the judges at the 50th anniversary of the AF Rayspeed 'S type' Lambretta. It was a very hard job as there were so many good scooters in this event.

People in middle of photograph Ron Moss, Dick Sedgley, Ray Kemp and Ben Kemp.

Dick Sedgley standing by a Royspeed at AF Rayspeed. Could this be the best scooter at this event! No, not on this occasion.

AF RAYSPEED 15/16/17 AUGUST 2015

Two photographs showing just a few of the vast amount of scooters and riders that turned up AF Rayspeed shop and field for the Anniversary of the Rayspeed S TYPE Scooters plus a fantastic firework display to music on the last evening.

Jan and I would like to thank Ray, Ben and their families for their hospitality over the weekend, we had a great time. Also meeting all their hardworking staff, Arthur Francis, John and Normand Ronald, and their wives, who we met at the evening meal.

Here I am sitting on my fully restored Lambretta Royspeed GP 150 with two other restored Lambretta scooters. I am wearing the GT 200 T-Shirt as I have the honour of being the president of the GT Lambretta Club after the sad loss of Mr. PJ Agg. All these Lambretta scooters are used on the road at different times.

LAST PAGE OF THIS BOOK

I have now reached the close of this book which holds my memories and journey of 60 years with Lambretta and so many friends I have made over this time.

Before I close the book, I must add only a small number of Lambretta machines suffered with the troubles mentioned in this book. Quite a few problems with Lambretta scooters were because of poor maintenance and repairs.

I would like to mention a few dealers I have dealt with over the years:

'Ricky Pitstop' Scooters shop, Romford, Essex.
Andy, Two-tones shop, Romford, Essex.
Dick, Bead Blasting Shop, South Ockendon, Essex.
Marko and Steve, Lambretta Spares, Essex.
Mauld and Patch, Scooter Surgery, London.
Peter and staff, Cambridge Lambrettas, St. Ives, Cambridge.
Ray, Mary, Ben and all the staff at AF Rayspeed, Yorkshire.
All great people with many thanks.

Hopefully, I will be riding my scooters for a few more years, and meeting up with friends from The Epsom Lambretta Club in Surrey, also the Specials and Fab Scooter Clubs, in Hornchurch, Essex.

Thank you to Peter Pooley who has helped with many issues and finding information. To Jan my wife for the hard work helping me produce the book.

Also, thanks to my daughter Stephanie for all her hard work getting my book ready for publication, after being let down very badly by people in the scootering world, which has delayed this publication. Also, Debbie my youngest daughter who helped by proofreading the book.

I hope people have enjoyed reading 'My Journey with Lambretta Scooters' through the years as much as I have enjoyed the experience and making so many friends.

HAPPY SCOOTERING.